THE DIGITAL PARENTING GUIDEBOOK

THE DIGITAL PARENTING GUIDEBOOK

7 Essential Steps for Building the Tech-Savvy Christian Family

DAVID TUCKER

DigitalParenting.com

TO MY DAD
*who showed me how to honor Christ
in this world through life and death.*

CONTENTS

BEFORE YOU READ

ALTHOUGH I HAVE EXTENSIVE EXPERIENCE with the technology powering our digital world and believe the content of this book teaches an effective and biblical way to keep technology from harming your family, if you have immediate concerns about your child's well-being, I recommend that you consult a professional.

Also, to help you understand the risks your family faces, I must address some difficult topics. This list includes anxiety, depression, suicide, abuse, pornography, sexual predators, and bullying. I will present true stories to illustrate these dangers. I understand that they may bring up painful memories. Please practice necessary self-care while reading this book.

1

Urgency

ON OCTOBER 22, 2021 a popular fifteen-year-old football player from Ohio, Braden Markus, sat at his computer, trying to finish a school assignment on a Sunday morning. As he made his way through his schoolwork, he was notified of a friend request on Instagram from an attractive girl around his age. This unexpected invitation quickly shifted his focus.

After a handful of direct messages, the girl requested that they switch the conversation over to Google Hangouts. Braden agreed. This new friend sent pictures of herself, and in return she asked Braden to reciprocate with nude pictures of himself. Braden repeatedly objected to the requests, but this girl was relentless. If Braden was slow to respond on Hangouts, she reverted to messaging him on Instagram. Eventually Braden gave in and sent one picture.

What Braden didn't know was that he wasn't interacting with a teenage girl at all. He was interacting with a predator who would blackmail him for profit. This predator compiled the content Braden sent into a video and threatened to post it to every porn site in the world. Braden was assured that this outcome was inevitable unless he paid $1,800 immediately. Braden panicked. He repeatedly begged the predator not to ruin his life. Just twenty-seven minutes after this initial friend request, Braden Markus took his own life.

Molly Russel, a fourteen-year-old girl from London, was heavily involved in social media, especially Instagram and Pinterest. She had been spending an ever-increasing amount of time on her phone. While her parents had noticed a change in her behavior, Molly had assured them that this was just a phase she was going through. What her parents didn't know was that there was an entire world Molly was keeping secret from them.

On what seemed like a normal fall morning in November 2017, Molly's mother noticed that her daughter hadn't yet emerged from her room, so she climbed the stairs to check on her. At 7 a.m. on November 21 she entered Molly's room to discover her child's lifeless body. At just fourteen years of age, Molly Russel was dead. Earlier that morning she had committed suicide.

In the aftermath of this tragedy, Molly's parents learned that their daughter was fixating on troubling content during her private screen time. In the six months leading up to her death, she had interacted with at least 2,100 pieces of content related to suicide, self-harm, and depression.[1] While conducting an inquest into Molly's death, it became difficult for some of the health professionals to sleep at night after reviewing this content.[2] While Molly was voraciously consuming this content, her parents had no idea of the darkness invading their daughter's mind.

I've read far too many stories like these. I grieve for all the young

---

1   Adam Satariano, "British Ruling Pins Blame on Social Media for Teenager's Suicide," *The New York Times*, October 1, 2022, https://www.nytimes.com/2022/10/01/business/instagram-suicide-ruling-britain.html.

2   Dan Milmo, "Psychiatrist 'unable to sleep' after seeing material viewed by Molly Russell," *The Guardian*, September 27, 2022, https://www.theguardian.com/uk-news/2022/sep/27/molly-russell-inquiry-hears-of-distressing-self-harm-content.

people like Braden who fall prey to those who wish to do them harm online. I also grieve for those like Molly, who go to social media to find friendship and connection; only to be met with pain and hopelessness. I grieve for the families whose lives have been forever scarred by the side effects of the current digital world. *All of these are tragedies.*

I'm not here to blame Braden's or Molly's families, and I'm not here to judge you either. Just as your child didn't come with a life instruction manual for technology, we didn't get one for parenting in this digital world. The fact remains that the dangers, which I'll be covering in this book, exist. The good news is that if you have a child under your care, you still have time to make a difference. It's not too late, but it is urgent.

THE BACKSTORY

Over the past decade, I've presented the dangers of technology to countless churches, schools, and civic groups. Inevitably I'll encounter three types of parents. First, I'll encounter the family that understands these risks clearly because they have already deeply wounded their household. It's not uncommon for a grieving mom or dad to approach me with tears in their eyes after an event. While they agree with what I've presented, they wish they had acted sooner to save their family from their current trauma. I want to spare you from falling into this category.

The second type of parent is enthusiastic about the content. They will have nothing but praise for what I've presented, but then they'll almost always respond with the same line: "I know someone who really needs this. I'll pass this information along to them." If I push them on this a bit, I learn that their own child is simply too smart and too good to fall prey to these dangers. They incorrectly believe that they are immune. I plead with you to not fall into this category.

The third type of parent is different. While they may not immediately agree with everything I have shared, they are eager to learn more. There is always a statistic, a story, or an insight from my presentation that they want to dive into. They may even have several questions about the specific devices they have in their home. They acknowledge the dangers, and they understand the urgency. I hope that each of you will fall into this category. I'm not asking you to blindly believe in this approach. Instead, I am asking you to look at the data and draw your own conclusions.

You may already have some preconceived notions about me. Am I some sort of technology-hating zealot who desires for everyone to put down their phones and return to life as it was in the 1990s? That couldn't be further from the truth. No one wants grunge music to make a comeback anyway.

Technology is deeply integrated into my life. I've spent my career writing software and helping some of the most well-known companies in the world with their digital strategies. I've written books, spoken at conferences, and created online courses on technical leadership and software development.

Throughout this time, I've also been involved in my church. My connection to technology made me a resource for families who were having digital struggles. Over time the word got out to other churches and groups. While these conversations with families were often difficult, they weren't unexpected. I know firsthand about some of the dangers that can come from technology.

I'm not here to shame anyone. I've had my own struggles that have affected my own family. Have you had seasons of life where you were on your phone constantly, even around your family? I have. Have you had your own struggles with digital temptations like pornography? I have. Have you ignored areas that could pose a danger for your family? I have too. This book is designed to present you with a framework for using technology wisely in your home: *The 7 Essential Steps of Digital Parenting.*

THIS BOOK IS FOR YOU

I know there will be many different types of people coming at this book from many different angles: parents who are concerned about how technology is affecting their child, grandparents who want to provide guidance to their grandchild, and even pastors looking to provide the families in their church with practical resources to help them deal with technology wisely. No matter what situation you are in, I believe this book can help you.

Next, this book is unapologetically Christian. I believe that any family can find value in *The 7 Essential Steps of Digital Parenting*, but you need to know that the underlying principles are from the Bible. If you aren't a Christian, please keep reading. I believe that there is still value for you here. As you read this book, I hope you will realize that these biblical principles, which have been around for thousands of years, are still applicable in today's digital world.

Throughout the book I'll use phrases like "your family" or "your child," but I realize not all of you fit that mold. It isn't always parents who have the greatest impact on a child's life. I believe many grandparents, aunts, uncles, foster parents, pastors, teachers, neighbors, and friends can play a critical role in protecting young people from the dangers that exist in this digital world—in fact, we need all hands on deck.

HARD TRUTHS

Before we get to the next chapter, I need to present you with some hard truths. I want you to have a realistic expectation of the digital world and how you can protect your family from its dangers. I also need to be up front about what this book can and cannot do for your family.

IT WILL TAKE WORK TO IMPLEMENT THE RECOMMENDATIONS IN THIS BOOK.

This book is not designed to be a theoretical resource. Consider this a repair guide, not a coffee table book. After most of the chapters in this book you will have homework assignments. These assignments will walk you through conversations I suggest you have with your child as well as boundaries you need to put in place. Assignments will even go beyond your child, as I'll be asking you to take a hard look at your own digital habits as well. While I will provide recommendations, you will have to decide what you will enforce in your home.

YOU CANNOT BLOCK EVERYTHING FROM YOUR CHILD.

In today's digital world, everyone seems to have a smartphone in their pocket, schools are handing out tablets in kindergarten, and social media has become the default means of communication. I wish there was a way that I could guarantee a safety bubble for your child, but this culture makes it impossible. In the United States more than 70% of twelve- and thirteen-year-olds have a smartphone.[3] Even if your child doesn't have one, chances are they will run into another kid who has one without any limits or filters. Whether at school, church, or around the neighborhood, your child will need to know how to make the right decision when faced with digital dangers and temptations.

THERE IS NO MAGIC TOOL THAT WILL SOLVE THIS FOR YOU.

Several years ago, I had a conversation with a friend whose daughter was in her early teen years. He was regretting getting her a smartphone. He told me, "I wish there was a way I could track everything she is doing without her knowing." Maybe you have pondered the same thing.

Real protection comes about by preparing your child for what they will encounter, then providing them with boundaries to limit their exposure. If you skip the hard conversations, you will skip an opportunity to

---

3   Victoria Rideout et al., *Common Sense Census: Media Use by Tweens and Teens* (San Francisco, CA: Common Sense, 2021), 22, https://www.commonsensemedia.org/research/the-common-sense-census-media-use-by-tweens-and-teens-2021.

walk beside your child as they grow. Digital parenting is a type of discipleship, and discipleship requires that you both teach your child what they should do and also model the behaviors you want them to adopt.

THE EARLIER YOU START, THE EASIER IT WILL BE.

I remember sitting in a church in rural Virginia, listening to a mom explain everything that had gone wrong in the life of her seventeen-year-old daughter because of technology. Up to that point, technology had gone completely unchecked in their home, and the mom was begging me for some quick solutions to undo half a decade of bad decisions. When things have been allowed to go unchecked for an extended period of time, things get more complicated. In many cases, professional help is required.

If this is your situation, there is still value in the principles contained in this book. If your child has already fully immersed themselves in the digital world without any guidance, implementing these principles will likely require some additional work. Because this may be the case for many of you, chapter 12 is dedicated to helping you evaluate whether professional help is necessary.

If you are very early in your parenting journey, I am thrilled. You are the reason this book exists. While I love helping families that are experiencing challenges, I envision an entire generation of families that will be spared the dangers brought about by technology because they implemented these concepts early in their child's life. This is why I get excited to work on this content every day.

HOW TO USE THIS BOOK

This book is designed to be used alongside the online resources we provide at DigitalParenting.com. Most chapters will open with a link that will get you to those resources. These resources include templates for plans you'll need to create, links to valuable tools you can use in your home, and even instructions for how to set up devices in your own home. Since that information needs to be updated often, we have included it on our website instead of in this book.

Maybe you picked up this book at a bookstore, an online retailer, or at your church. By pairing it with the online resources, you will have what you need to implement *The 7 Essential Steps of Digital Parenting* covered in these pages. While you can navigate this content on your own, it is even better if you have a friend or family member join in. There are topics and concepts that you'll likely want to discuss with someone else.

There is also another way you can navigate this content. At DigitalParenting.com we have created a course, *Digital Parenting Fundamentals*, that can be used to help groups walk through this content together. We have found that building a parenting community around *The 7 Essential Steps of Digital Parenting* provides both support and accountability when it comes to implementing the steps in your home. We equip churches to offer this course as a class or small group study.

Even if you are walking through this book alone, you can still be a part of a community. We have created the *Digital Parenting Community* to help like-minded parents share their questions and experiences while implementing the recommendations in this book. If you visit DigitalParenting.com and click on the Community link, you can join in the discussions.

We've got a lot to get to, so let's dive in!

PART I

The Foundation

2

The Role of Technology

ON MOST SUNDAY AFTERNOONS my family and I load up after church and head to my in-laws' farm on the outskirts of the Cherokee National Forest. Afternoons at the farm are filled with food, board games, and visits with the many animals my in-laws have acquired over the years. As the adults sit at the kitchen table and talk after Sunday afternoon lunch, we are just as likely to see a horse and buggy pass by their picture window as we are a car. This is because my in-laws live directly next to a Mennonite community nestled in the hills of East Tennessee.

Watching them ride by, a momentary feeling of jealousy overcomes me. They don't have to worry about notifications, online trends, or whether they remembered to post happy birthday to a family member on social media. It appears that there is something in our inherently busied digital world that wars against the simplicity our hearts desire. In moments like this, I'm quick to remember the blessings of air conditioning, video calls with friends around the globe, and the ability to text my wife when I have a question at the grocery store.

Before we dive too deep into looking at how our families can engage with technology in a beneficial way, it is worth asking ourselves whether we should even try. Are smartphones so problematic that we should avoid them altogether? Does the existence of Internet pornography mean that we should shun the web altogether?

WALKING WISELY

If we look in the Bible at the book of Exodus, we can examine two events that happened during the lifetime of Moses. In the first event we can see the people of Israel following God's instructions to construct the tabernacle.[1] Once built, this tabernacle was where God would meet with His people. It must have been a sight to behold as the glory of the Lord filled the tabernacle once all the intricate wood, metal, and textile work had been completed.

Just a few chapters earlier, we see a very different use of these skills. As the people of Israel waited for Moses to come down from Mount Sinai, they chose to abandon their obedience to God and create an idol, a golden calf.[2] Eventually Moses came down from the mountain and confronted their grievous sin. Given the metal work required to form both the golden calf and the tabernacle, the same tools were likely used for both. Once for obedience, and once for disobedience.

Technology works in the same way. It has the power to save lives, extend ministry, and enrich learning. When misused it can enslave us to sin, enable abuse, and distract us from the truth. While technology is a tool that can be used for both good and evil, its potential for both is greater than most other tools. How do we reconcile our use of this tool with our calling as Christians and our roles as parents, guardians, family members, and friends?

Paul tells the church at Ephesus, "Look carefully then how you walk, not as unwise but as wise, making the best use of the time,

---

1   See Exod 35:30–40:38.

2   See Exod 32.

because the days are evil" (Ephesians 5:15–16). While this passage seems relatively straightforward, there are some profound truths that we can extract from it.

First, Paul is telling us that there is a way we can live our lives that is wise while there is another that is unwise. This means that all areas of our lives should be closely examined to see which side we are on. Our technology intersects with so many other parts of our lives that it certainly deserves some analysis.

Next, Paul tells us that we are to make the best use of our time. Even in the first century, Paul was pleading with Christians to think about what was ultimately beneficial when it came to the use of their time. You may already be squirming a bit with this one. Many of us are spending much more time staring at screens than we would like to admit. If we evaluate our pervasive use of social media and online entertainment, it should lead us to ask, "Is this the best use of our time?"

Finally, Paul tells the church, "The days are evil." That's just as true today as it was in 62 AD, when Paul penned these words. If we simply go with the flow of our culture, we may be guilty of falling into this evil as well. This is a call for us to never blindly accept anything, simply because it is the trend of the day. We are called to be intentional about how we live, and in many cases that will mean choosing a countercultural approach. Chapter 3 is focused on exploring this concept at a deeper level.

Tony Reinke, Christian author and journalist, authored *God, Technology, and the Christian Life* in which he seeks to analyze the ways in which Christians should and should not engage with technology. As he reflects on the implications of 1 Timothy 4:4–5 in relation to technology, he says: "If we can honestly thank God for it, we can adopt it . . . Christ teaches us to be thankful for the innovations we need and content without the ones we don't."[3]

We are called to take an honest look at what is wise and what is

---

3   Tony Reinke, *God, Technology, and the Christian Life* (London: Crossway, 2022), 292.

unwise. This will likely mean that there will be some new digital trends we will adopt as well as others we will not. As Tony says, we must learn to be content without those things we do not believe are wise for ourselves and our families.

In most places where I speak, there is at least one family who has decided to abandon almost all technology in their homes. I understand this reaction and, quite frankly, sometimes it may even be the best course of action. This leads to the first key insight:

If you don't have the time or desire to educate and protect your family when it comes to technology, you would be better off forgoing it altogether.

I truly mean that. Get phones without Internet capabilities, get your media from an antenna, read physical books, and don't even think about an Internet connection at home. This won't fix everything, but it will prevent some of the biggest dangers from entering your home.

However, this approach is not without its flaws. There are few places left in this world where your child won't encounter someone who has completely unrestricted access to everything on the Internet: the good and the bad. Most schools have computers students can use, and while they generally have some protections, teens are remarkably savvy at evading them. We can't control their environment forever and at some point, they will be confronted with situations that will require responsible and biblical decisions on their part—and we need to prepare them for that.

THE CASE FOR TECHNOLOGY

One Monday night I decided to watch an American football game while cleaning up my home office. After clearing some books off my desk, I pulled the game up on my iPad. I was met with something completely unexpected. Instead of the typical flurry of activity that makes up an NFL game, I was met by an image of an ambulance parked in the middle of the field. I quickly stopped cleaning, sat down in my office chair, and tried to get a better sense of what had just happened.

During the game one of the players, Damar Hamlin, had collapsed after suffering cardiac arrest immediately following a tackle. The announcers informed the audience that CPR was being performed on the player while the other players from both teams were seen praying for him. Many of these players had tears in their eyes.

As I write this chapter, Damar is well on his way to recovery. He has been discharged from the hospital—something that seemed unthinkable during the chaos that Monday night in Cincinnati. We have also learned more about the measures that were leveraged to truly save his life in the moments following his collapse. One essential piece of equipment that was used was a portable automated external defibrillator (AED).

Because of advancements in technology, these units are no longer limited to hospitals. They now just weigh a few pounds and—while still not cheap—they are now affordable enough that many businesses, community centers, schools, and churches have mounted them on their walls. These units have been optimized to give verbal commands to those administering care, based on the patient's vital signs, which are monitored continually during use by sensors that are placed on the patient's body. Previously, it required a professional with medical training to operate such a device. Now anyone can do it.

I believe that this is just one example of how advancements in technology can be an example of God's grace to us. I've seen technology help families communicate more frequently, missionaries spread the story of Jesus more easily, businesses work more efficiently, and even governments operate more transparently. There are many examples of God's grace in the technology we experience daily when it is used wisely.

It is also true that the research I'll cover in this book connects some of our technological advancements with things we would never want to see happen in our families. This brings me to another key insight for all families:

If you bring technology into your home, you must provide the necessary guidance and boundaries to keep it from harming your relationships with God and each other.

I realize the gravity of this statement. According to Pew Research, 66% of parents in the United States say that parenting now is harder than it was twenty years ago.[4] What was the leading reason they gave for this? You guessed it: technology. The good news is that you are not alone. Most every parent I speak with is scrambling to deal with an ever-changing set of digital challenges.

CORE BELIEFS

I founded DigitalParenting.com to help families use technology for its benefits while avoiding the ever-growing list of dangers it presents. In full transparency, I'd like to present you with the core beliefs that undergird this book, our online resources, and our live events. I don't ever want to hide the beliefs that govern how we do things and shape the resources we create:

1. **The Bible is the source of truth and an infallible parenting guide.** We believe the Bible, not the current age, is a steady and reliable guide.

2. **Technology can be used for both good and evil.** Rather than shun all technology, we believe in using it in obedience to God's commands.

3. **Peer-reviewed research is a source of valuable insight.** We believe proven research is essential to understanding the challenges posed by technology.

---

4   Brooke Auxier et al., "Parenting Children in the Age of Screens," *Pew Research Center,* July 28, 2020, https://www.pewresearch.org/internet/2020/07/28/parenting-children-in-the-age-of-screens/.

4. **Discipleship is the key to success.** We believe that tools can only go so far. Effective teaching is how we will ultimately combat the harms of technology.

With these core beliefs in place, I created *The 7 Essential Steps of Digital Parenting* to give parents an easy-to-follow framework for protecting their families. Before I explain these seven steps to you, let's chat about the calling we have as parents and what it truly means to be countercultural.

3

Countercultural

THE LONG ROOM of the Old Library at Trinity College, Dublin, is a sight to behold. Walking down the hardwood corridor feels like a journey into the past. The 200,000 volumes stored in this room seem to stretch as far as the eye can see. The bookshelves are so tall that ladders are required to reach those delicate ancient volumes sitting twenty feet above the floor. Marble busts of scholars, poets, and nobles adorn the pathway through this trove of knowledge.

I remained in a state of awe until I accidentally bumped into a couple in front of me. As I snapped back into reality, I noticed that they were setting up for a selfie. I apologized and quickly moved to not interrupt their Instagram moment. Throughout my visit, I kept an eye on this couple. They took at least seven selfies. They never stopped to read any of the details about the library; they never examined the bookshelves; they never stopped to view any of the marble busts. They came for their pictures, and then they left.

As I looked around, I noticed that more than half of those navigating this architectural masterpiece were more concerned with the pictures they were taking of this experience than they were with the experience itself. Some visitors took the time to take in every plaque and exhibit detailing the storied history of the building, but those people were in the minority.

Don't worry. I'm not starting a war on selfies. I bring this up because it is a metaphor for what it is like to be countercultural in a world obsessed with going all-in on technology. If you follow the recommendations in this book, you will be different. Other parents will notice; your child will notice; your extended family will notice. You will likely get pushback from some unexpected places. While I wish I could spare you from this reality, it will happen anytime someone chooses to not follow the crowd. To deal with this difficult reality, it is important for us to understand the calling we have been given by God as parents.

FOR SUCH A TIME AS THIS

In the Old Testament book of Esther, the story is told of a young woman who saved the people of Israel from destruction. Even though God is not mentioned directly in this book, it is evident that He is ultimately working through several characters in this historical account. But in the moment, it was hard for Esther to see this.

Esther was a Jewish orphan who was being raised by her uncle, Mordecai. When King Ahasuerus was looking for a new queen, he chose her from among all the women who had been gathered from his kingdom. She was now living in the palace with all of its luxuries. Meanwhile her uncle Mordecai learned that the king's right-hand man, Haman, was plotting to destroy the Jews.

Mordecai passed this information on to Esther through various members of the king's household. Esther was initially hesitant to go to the king and address this plot. Anyone who came to the king uninvited risked losing their life, even Esther. Mordecai reminded Esther of the gravity of the situation for all the Jews. He told her, "And who knows whether you have not come to the kingdom for such a time as this?"[1]

---

1   See Esth 4:14b.

Mordecai's message was clear. God was working, and Esther was exactly where God wanted her to be to prevent this atrocity. Because of Esther's obedience, the Jews were saved, Haman was hanged, and Mordecai took over Haman's position of authority.

It is no accident that you are a parent, a grandparent, a concerned family member, or a pastor today. God has chosen you to be alive in this age to prevent harm to the people you love. Instead of spending our energy wishing things were different, let's embrace this truth.

With this understanding, we can also embrace the promises that God gives us in His word. Paul tells the church at Philippi, "And my God will supply every need of yours according to his riches in glory in Christ Jesus."[2] I believe this promise is just as true for you today as it was when it was written.

If we bring these truths together, we have another key insight that should define our perspective for the current age we find ourselves in:

*If God has called you to be a parent, guardian,
or leader in this digital world, he will provide what
you need to accomplish what he has called you to do.*

AGAINST THE GRAIN

In a return visit to a church in Virginia, I decided to meet with some parents who were already implementing aspects of digital parenting in their own homes. I wanted to get feedback on what they were experiencing. During this meeting I asked them about any pushback they had received while implementing my recommendations. To my surprise the major source of pushback wasn't their child, it was other parents.

When you take a proactive approach to protecting your child from digital dangers, friends and family members may feel that you are judging their decisions when it comes to topics like screen time. Grandparents

---

2   See Phil 4:19.

may feel that you are micromanaging what they can do while they are spending time with their grandchild. Neighbors may even believe you are being immoral for trying to limit your child's self-expression on the Internet. While these objections may cause some relational tensions, it doesn't change the calling we have been given to be wise parents.

In Romans 12 we are told to "not be conformed to this world, but be transformed by the renewal of your mind, that by testing you may discern what is the will of God, what is good and acceptable and perfect."[3] This verse calls us to become analyzers of our culture who can discern what God wants us to do within our cultural context. If we see a behavior and see that it isn't good, acceptable, and perfect, then we should reject it. There are many online patterns of behavior that clearly don't fit these criteria.

I don't want this countercultural perspective to seem like it is all negative. When you embrace being countercultural you can recapture time your family may have spent just looking at screens, be present for more conversations with your spouse and child, and grow closer to God, spending more time in prayer and less time on social media. There are many benefits, but they will require you to seek approval from your creator, not your culture.

I want to prepare you for what it will take to implement digital changes in your home. This brings us to another key insight:

> *God, not man, should be where we seek approval*
> *when it comes to our digital habits. We will have to*
> *be countercultural to be obedient to His calling.*

A CITY ON A HILL

In 260 AD the plague of Cyprian had gripped the Roman Empire, and it wouldn't be eliminated for another decade. Everyone from Ethiopia

---

3   See Rom 12:2.

to Rome was terrified of the dreaded disease. But instead of running away from those afflicted by the disease, Christians were running toward them. Dionysius, the Bishop of Alexandria, observed that, "Heedless of danger, they took charge of the sick, attending to their every need and ministering to them in Christ, and with them departed this life serenely happy."[4] If you look at every plague that has afflicted the world from that time on, you'll find followers of Jesus at the forefront, responding to the needs of the afflicted.

While they might not admit it or even realize it, your neighbors, co-workers, extended family members, and friends are also struggling with the side effects of a technology-saturated culture. Side effects from technology's dangers are causing pain in a majority of homes. Many have just accepted these struggles as a part of modern life.

What if the church could be a beacon of maturity and restraint (when it comes to technology) that gives hope to those around us? What if we could follow Jesus's teaching and be the "city set on a hill"[5] for all to see? Being countercultural is not something we do *against* the world, it is something we do *for* the world. By being countercultural, we can show others that there is a better way. This brings us to the final key insight of this chapter:

By following biblical principles for how we use technology,
we can provide hope for all of those around us who
are dealing with the side effects of its misuse.

---

4   Moses Y. Lee, "What the Early Church Can Teach Us About the Coronavirus," *The Gospel Coalition* (blog), March 12, 2020, https://www.thegospelcoalition.org/article/what-early-church-teach-coronavirus/.

5   See Matt 5:14.

4

The Blueprint

IT'S TAKEN YOU YEARS, but you and your spouse have come up with the perfect design for your dream home. You've planned every room, optimized its layout, and even picked out the paint colors. To make this vision a reality, you have worked with an architect to create a blueprint, and this blueprint perfectly captures all your domestic dreams. It's got that massive garage to store your cars, a butler's pantry for all of your dry goods, and even a large game room your family can enjoy. After a long search, you have selected the contractor who will manage all aspects of the construction. Excited, you hand over the blueprint and wait for the house to be built.

When the day arrives to view your finished home, you and your spouse cannot contain your excitement. You both wake up before the alarm clock, eager to see your vision brought to life. As you make your way down the tree-lined drive to your new home, you gasp. Something has gone horribly wrong. Your home is missing two dormers, the paint colors are wrong, and the garage is half the expected size.

When you both approach the contractor, he can tell that you are furious. He assures you that when you handed over the blueprint eight months ago, he studied it meticulously. You scoff at this statement and remind him of the laundry list of requests he left out of the build. As you go down the list, you can see a hint of realization in his eyes as he remembers that those details were included in the original blueprint. In a defeated response, he tells you that between ordering materials, scheduling subcontractors, and applying for permits, he just didn't have time to revisit the blueprint during construction.

I realize this seems like a ridiculous illustration. You're likely thinking this could never happen in the real world, but this isn't a story about home building; it's a story about parenting. You likely have many "I want" statements that relate to your child and your family. Whether or not you have written them down, these represent your *parenting blueprint*. Maybe you have wants for how you will raise your child, the kind of environment you will create in your home, and what you will teach your child to become.

On a given day, you may wake up, make sure that school project is packed in the car, drop the kids off at school, head to work, pick up the kids after school, grab some groceries, hit the drive-thru for dinner, and then make sure to get the kids to their soccer practice on time. When you get home, you barely have time to make sure homework is done before you send the kids to bed and get ready to do it again the next day. Even if you set out with the best of intentions, at some point, you just shifted to survival mode, and left your blueprint to gather dust. How do we move past short-term survival and shift into intentional parenting?

To accomplish this, we must never, ever lose sight of the *wants* that make up our parenting blueprint. If you don't take time to define your wants, you'll be stuck in a rut, dealing with the things that seem urgent but don't really add long-term value to your family. Once you've defined your parenting blueprint, you can take any decision that comes your way and weigh it against your desired long-term outcomes. When you look at it this way, you will be surprised at how many things you can forego in order to regain the time to accomplish what is most important for you and your family.

Never lose sight of your parenting blueprint, which is made up of the wants you have for your family.

Your parenting blueprint is your own. I can't define it for you. Every family will need to determine the wants that make up this guide. To help you, I want to walk you through how we arrived at ours.

OUR WANTS

I will always remember the moment in November of 2008, when a delivery room nurse requested that I wheel the bassinet containing my newborn twin boys down to the labor and delivery nursery. In this moment, standing in one of the delivery rooms at Memorial Hospital in Savannah, Georgia, my new responsibility hit me like a ton of bricks. It was no longer the responsibility of a nurse or doctor to care for these boys; it was our responsibility as parents. While my wife Shannon and I had done a great deal to prepare for this moment, there was nothing that could have prepared me for that wave of emotions.

In the years that followed, we continued the discussion around how we would raise our children. We didn't always write things down, but we agreed on the *wants* that made up the blueprint for our home. I have consolidated these years of discussion into five wants that define what we want for our family. I don't expect you to adopt these, I'm just presenting them as an example. Ultimately, your wants are yours to define.

WE WANT OUR CHILDREN TO HAVE AN EVER-GROWING RELATIONSHIP WITH GOD.

Growing up in the '90s, most of my friends attended church. After heading to college, many of them abandoned their faith completely. As social media began to emerge, I was surprised to see that many of the people I had lost contact with over the years were living radically different lives than I would have expected. It was obvious that so many of them had been caught up in the cultural elements of Christianity without truly being connected to their creator.

I believe there is a reason why perseverance and endurance are considered markers of faithful followers of Jesus. Hebrews 3:14 tells us, "For we have come to share in Christ, if indeed we hold our original confidence firm to the end." We want to have children who hold firm until the end. We want to model a faith for them that perseveres despite difficulty.

IF OUR CHILDREN CHOOSE TO MARRY, WE WANT THEM TO HAVE STRONG MARRIAGES.

We realize that any of our children may feel called to be single, but if they do get married, we want their marriages to be built on a firm biblical foundation. Between my birth in 1981 and my twentieth birthday, divorce rates in the U.S. rose considerably. In the course of my children's lifetimes they have already seen the concept of lifelong marriage significantly decrease in popularity. In today's Western culture, the deck is stacked against the biblical concept of covenantal monogamy. This worries me for their sake.

No other human relationship has affected me like my marriage has. I have been blessed to have a wife who has pushed me to grow in Christ ever since we got married in 2005. If I look at the obstacles I've faced, I am amazed at how God has used her to support me during my darkest days. Her encouragement has given me the freedom to pursue God and follow him wherever he leads me.

We pray that our kids will find someone who supports them in a like manner. We want them to be prepared to work to maintain a relationship like that, and we pray that God will give them wisdom in their choice of a future spouse.

WE WANT OUR CHILDREN TO HAVE STRONG RELATIONSHIPS WITH THEIR FAMILY AND FRIENDS.

In Ecclesiastes 4:9–10 we see that, "Two are better than one, because they have a good reward for their toil. For if they fall, one will lift up his fellow. But woe to him who is alone when he falls and has not another to lift him up." I've been amazed at how God has used others to support me in difficult times. It's been a comfort to not walk through those times alone.

When we think of our kids, we want them to seek out strong, mutually supportive friendships rooted in a strong faith. We all have surface-level relationships with neighbors, fellow church members, and family, but we want them to seek out and nurture deeper and stronger relationships than that. Quantity isn't nearly as important as quality here. We all need someone to pick us up when we fall, and that takes a lot more than just a like on an Instagram post.

WE WANT OUR CHILDREN TO UNDERSTAND THE VALUE AND PURPOSE OF WORK.

In today's Western society, most professions are evaluated solely based on how much money they bring in. If someone has found a way to become wealthy, there is no need to ask whether their chosen profession is ultimately beneficial to society. In addition, many have come to believe that there is a certain amount of personal sacrifice that must be made to succeed professionally, which may include a failed marriage or a strained relationship with their kids.

As Christians, we should have the healthiest perspective on the value of work because we see our work as a continuation of God's work on earth. Dr. Tim Keller, the late pastor and best-selling author, stated that:

> We are continuing God's work of forming, filling, and subduing. Whenever we bring order out of chaos, whenever we draw out creative potential, whenever we elaborate and "unfold" creation beyond where it was when we found it, we are following God's pattern of creative cultural development.[1]

---

1   Timothy Keller, *Every Good Endeavor: Connecting Your Work to God's Work* (New York: Penguin Books, 2014), 48.

Advancing scientific understanding, healing illnesses, writing music, and teaching philosophy are all examples of work that adds value to society. We also want them to understand that while they should strive to grow in excellence at whatever they choose to do, their fulfillment is not based on their performance but rather on their identity in Christ.

WE WANT OUR CHILDREN TO BE CONTENT.

The world is full of sights we will never see, dreams we will never realize, and skills we will never perfect. We want our children to live in a state of contentment during their time in this world. To properly teach them this habit, my wife and I need to train them to focus on the blessings they have received instead of obsessing over the things they still desire.

My hope is that they will live out what the Apostle Paul taught in his letter to the church at Philippi:

> I am not saying this because I am in need, for I have learned to be content whatever the circumstances. I know what it is to be in need, and I know what it is to have plenty. I have learned the secret of being content in any and every situation, whether well fed or hungry, whether living in plenty or in want. (Philippians 4:11–12)

We don't want our children to confuse contentment with laziness, disinterest, or fear. No one ever accused the Apostle Paul of being lazy, but he was content with whatever situation God had placed him in. Contentment isn't a reason to stop exploring, learning, and experiencing areas of interest in this world. We want our children to pursue their areas of interest while remembering that their faith provides them with a relationship with Jesus, which is the only thing they ultimately need.

WHAT'S AT STAKE

This isn't a book on establishing an overall blueprint for your parenting, but I do think that having a blueprint is crucial to understanding why it is so important to address technology in your home. Later in my parenting journey, when I first began to research the impacts of technology, I learned that **every single one of the *wants* I had for my children was being threatened by technology**. This wasn't just conjecture; I was finding academic studies and personal stories that backed this up, (and many of these studies are referenced in the footnotes of this book). I want to walk you through some of my initial observations after reviewing this information, as well as connect it to some things you may want for your family.

Do you want your child to have a growing relationship with God? If you are a follower of Christ, I think you would agree that the ability to pray and study Scripture is paramount to this process. What if a continual stream of short-form video posts and a lack of periods of silence is destroying your child's ability to focus deeply on spiritual concepts?

Do you want your child to work on what is truly important in life? The average teen is spending between three and four years of their life between the ages of eight and eighteen playing video games, engaging on social media, and watching videos online. We are letting our children become addicted to continual micro-entertainment, filling every spare moment of their lives with meaningless, low-value content. Instead of building skills or gaining knowledge to serve others, we are ignoring the needs of the world so that we can binge watch the latest hit streaming show.

Do you want your child to have strong relationships? As relationships are now quantifiable on social media by the number of likes a person receives, friendships are lacking depth.[2] As teens spend more

---

2   Arthur C. Brooks, "Technology Can Make Your Relationships Shallower," *The Atlantic*, September 29, 2022, https://www.theatlantic.com/family/archive/2022/09/technology-happiness-communication-relationships/671586/.

time in front of screens, the face-to-face time required to build strong relationships is decreasing.

Do you want your child to have a strong marriage? With young people experiencing pornography at younger and younger ages, most everyone is coming into marriage with sexual baggage that has rarely been addressed. In addition, far too many teens have engaged not just in watching pornography, but also in creating it.

Do you want your child to know how to be content? We have seen a dramatic increase in depression, anxiety, and suicide among teens since we gave them all smartphones. It seems that the very presence of these devices is radically changing their perspective on their own lives.

At this point, you are likely asking for proof of my claims. You might already agree with some of these assertions, but you may vehemently disagree with others. I'll be walking you through the research and reasoning behind this analysis in the next section of this book.

YOUR BLUEPRINT

Whether you are a single parent, a couple, a grandparent, or a foster parent, I encourage you to take thirty minutes and write out your *wants* for the child entrusted to your care. Maybe your *wants* will be similar to ours or maybe you have other areas you'd like to focus on. I realize you could easily spend hours or days working on this, but I don't want to slow down your process of getting to Part II of this book. If you are reading through this with your spouse, I suggest you do this exercise together.

Once you have your wants in place, keep this parenting blueprint handy as you navigate through *The 7 Essential Steps of Digital Parenting*. Whenever you read a statistic or learn about a risk related to your wants, be sure to take note. While I hope that our wants will inspire you, I want you to make this exercise your own.

Of course, your blueprint doesn't have to remain static. After this first thirty minutes, you can continue to tweak it until you feel that it adequately captures the things you want for your family. But don't let perfection get in the way of progress here. The point is to get started. I've yet to meet a family that created a perfect parenting blueprint in a single sitting.

> *Once your parenting blueprint is firmly in place, you*
> *can move forward to Part II, where we will explore*
> The 7 Essential Steps of Digital Parenting.

PART II

The 7 Essential Steps of Digital Parenting

Action Plan Tracker Worksheet: https://dp.run/track

With a draft of your parenting blueprint in place, we can move forward to the core of the book. In Part II I will walk you through *The 7 Essential Steps of Digital Parenting*. While these steps are each unique, they do have a few things in common.

First, I want you to understand that following the order of these steps matters. Every step is critical, but I have tackled the most important ones first. In addition, the benefits you will gain from each step are cumulative. For example, the tasks you complete in Step 1 will help protect your child from the dangers discussed in Step 4.

Second, each step has an Action Plan associated with it, containing multiple tasks you will need to complete. These tasks range from leading your child through a Bible study to having a guided discussion about a digital parenting topic to implementing a specific plan to address an area of concern. Using the printable worksheet that can be found at the link above, you can track your efforts across all of these tasks.

Next, there are additional resources available for each step online. The templates, discussion guides, and Bible studies I'll refer to can all be found in these online resources. The link to the online resources will be included in the Action Plan for each of the steps.

Finally, if you aren't a part of a small group or class going through this material, you may feel like you are stranded on an island. But you don't have to figure all of this out on your own. As I mentioned earlier, we launched the *Digital Parenting Community* so that parents could have a place to ask questions, get input, and connect with other parents who are on the same journey. I encourage you to take a few minutes now and join the community. Just navigate to DigitalParenting.com and click on the Community link.

Special Needs

Every parent will need to customize the recommendations in this book for their family, but I realize that for some families this may prove challenging. I have spoken with many families who have seen the benefits of technology in the life of their special needs child. For example, I have seen children with severe autism find community in online spaces when it seemed nearly impossible for them to do so in a face-to-face setting.

In situations like these, I recommend parents use their spiritual discernment paired with professional counsel. Any medical or mental health professional currently treating your child can provide valuable input on the plan you are creating throughout this book. While every topic covered in this book still needs to be addressed, I recognize that some of the decisions you make regarding your Action Plan will be uniquely tailored to your child.

5

STEP 1

Regulating Screen Time

So teach us to number our days that we may get a heart of wisdom.
(PSALM 90:12)

MY FIRST MEMORY of a video game was playing a title called *Adventure* on our 8-bit Atari 2600 video game console. The main character was nothing more than a square on the screen that you navigated using the console's single-button joystick. To beat the game, you had to avoid three different dragons, which looked more like ducks, given the 8-bit graphics. The entire game could be completed in roughly fifteen minutes, although it generally took quite a bit longer to figure out the various puzzles that had to be solved. On any given day in my first-grade year,

37

I spent ten or twenty minutes playing this game, then I went outside to ride my bike.

In the fall of 2002, I was navigating my college schedule as an upperclassman at Middle Tennessee State University. In the off-campus apartment I shared with two friends from my hometown, we had multiple video game consoles. Between *Halo* and *Morrowind*, the Xbox was running continuously. When one of us returned from class, we took over from the roommate who was getting ready to head to campus.

Unlike the 8-bit games of my early childhood, these games were immersive and addictive. I started to notice that during class my thoughts would wander from the lecture hall to the living room of our apartment. I was plotting and planning how to conquer the next challenge of whatever game I was playing at the time. For the first time in my life, I began to understand the allure that could come from staring at a screen, and I was starting to realize that it could have negative impacts on my life.

If we fast-forward to the present time, the challenges have increased dramatically. The temptation to get caught up in the latest video game or social media trend has shifted from the living room to our pockets. A generation born into the digital world is trying to navigate technologies they did not invent. In many cases, they were given devices in their strollers. They weren't twenty when digital platforms began to creep into their thoughts; they were seven. In many ways the deck has been stacked against them, and many do not yet realize how it is affecting them. It's all they have ever known.

Look at your parenting blueprint. I want you to remember your *wants* as we walk through the dangers associated with excessive screen time. While many view screen time as a harmless distraction, there is more at risk than you may know. I suspect many of you think I am blowing the dangers of screen time out of proportion, but let's take a step back and explore the data together.

A Definition

Before we get too deep into this chapter, let's define *screen time*. For the purposes of this book, our working definition will be:

Screen Time: Any time spent interacting with a screen-based device.

I realize that this definition may seem overly simplistic, but it has some huge ramifications. If your child is doing school work online, that is screen time. If your child is playing a game on your phone while waiting at the doctor's office, that is screen time. If your child watches TV with the family, that is screen time. You can only get a true picture of the total amount of screen time you and your child are consuming if you include all of its forms.

What Young People Are Doing

Your child is being raised as a native of the digital world. There are vast differences between what digital natives do and don't do with their time, compared to previous generations. If you think that's a big deal, you are not alone. If anyone says that they know exactly how this will affect your child, they are lying to you. The effects of this massive shift will take decades to fully understand.

The biggest addition to the schedule of today's youth comes as no surprise: screen time has continued to increase since the inception of the smartphone. While screen time isn't a new concept, the types of screen-based activities have changed from generation to generation.

Common Sense, a secular nonprofit that provides research and reviews pertaining to our digital world, released The Common Sense Census in 2021.[1] This study provides essential data to help us understand how tweens and teens spend their screen time in the United States. While this research covers many aspects of their online behavior, I'll

---

1   Rideout et al., *Common Sense Census*, 13.

be focusing on one specific area: the amount of time spent on various digital activities per day.

To help us understand the weight of the numbers presented in this study, I want to extrapolate what the life of an average eight-year-old looks like up through the time they are eighteen. As we look at the results of this study, I hope that many of you will realize that this presents a significant departure from your teen years.

Activity	Average Daily Time (Ages 8-12)	Average Daily Time (Ages 13-18)	Total Hours (Ages 8-18)
TV / Online Videos	2 hrs 40 mins	3 hrs 16 mins	12,021
Gaming	1 hr 27 mins	1 hr 46 mins	6,515
Browsing	24 mins	51 mins	2,592
Social Media	18 mins	1 hr 27 mins	3,723
Content Creation	8 mins	14 mins	754
Video Chatting	12 mins	20 mins	1,095
Total Hours			26,700 Hours
Total Duration			4 years 208 days

Figure 1: Cumulative time spent during the tween and teen years (ages 8–18) based on data from the 2021 Common Sense Census[2]

Within these categories, the average teen is spending more than four and a half years of their waking hours at home on screen-based entertainment activities. This isn't the outlier. This is the average. Remember, there are some teens with numbers that far exceed these. During their formative years, when today's youth should be building a spiritual and educational

---

2   This figure utilizes the previously cited study, *The Common Sense Census*. When the total duration is calculated, it is based on 16 waking hours per day. The sum per category is based on the daily averages provided by the study.

foundation that will support them as they head out into the world, they are instead investing in activities that provide only temporary value.

What Young People Aren't Doing

I want you to stop and think about what this amount of screen time means for your child. They didn't just find more hours in the day for technology. What has been removed to make room for this glut of screen time?

One area where the data demonstrates a shift is both in the quality and quantity of sleep. Teens today are taking longer to fall asleep, having a harder time getting up in the morning, struggling with more sleepiness throughout the day, and experiencing lower energy levels overall.[3] At face value, these effects are already problematic, but the emotional and mental health ramifications are potentially catastrophic. I'll be addressing mental health at a much deeper level once we get to Step 3, which I'll be covering in chapter 7.

Another shift is from in-person social interactions to virtual communication. Dr. Jean Twenge wrote, "In the late 1970s, 52 percent of 12th-graders got together with their friends almost every day. By 2017, only 28 percent did. The drop was especially pronounced after 2010."[4] This date ties in closely with the time smartphones were shifting from being toys for early tech adopters to becoming a vital part of mainstream culture.

Leisure reading has also taken a hit. The number of thirteen-year-olds who read "almost every day" has been cut in half since 1984. While this may seem like teens are simply trading one form of entertainment for another, it is important to remember the role that reading and comprehension play in the life of Christ followers, responsible citizens, and future leaders.

---

3   Sylvie Royant-Parola et al., "The Use of Social Media Modifies Teenagers' Sleep-Related Behavior," *L'Encéphale* 44, no. 4 (2018), 321–328. doi:10.1016/j.encep.2017.03.009.

4   Jean Twenge, "Teens Have Less Face Time with Their Friends – and Are Lonelier than Ever," *The Conversation*, March 20, 2019, https://theconversation.com/teens-have-less-face-time-with-their-friends-and-are-lonelier-than-ever-113240.

Dr. Maryanne Wolf, a scholar and literacy advocate, detailed her concern for society in a 2018 article for *The Guardian*. In preparation for this article she reviewed current research and even spoke with teachers and professors about their own experiences in today's classrooms. Her conclusions point to far-reaching consequences for today's young people, who have spent most of their time in school skimming passages instead of thoroughly analyzing texts.

> English literature scholar and teacher Mark Edmundson describes how many college students actively avoid the classic literature of the 19th and 20th centuries because they no longer have the patience to read longer, denser, more difficult texts. We should be less concerned with students' "cognitive impatience," however, than by what may underlie it: the potential inability of large numbers of students to read with a level of critical analysis sufficient to comprehend the complexity of thought and argument found in more demanding texts, whether in literature and science in college, or in wills, contracts and the deliberately confusing public referendum questions citizens encounter in the voting booth.[5]

Followers of Christ should realize that the Bible fits into this category of "longer, denser, more difficult texts" that Dr. Wolf is referring to. Ask anyone who has been teaching young people in church for over a decade if they have seen a decline in biblical literacy and comprehension. I have yet to speak to one of them who hasn't.

You should be concerned about what your child's generation is doing with their digital devices, but I hope you can see that it is equally important to recognize what they're not doing. By not connecting face-to-face with friends, getting a full night's sleep, diving into a physical

---

5   Maryanne Wolf, "Skim Reading Is the New Normal. The Effect on Society Is Profound," *The Guardian*, August 25, 2018, https://www.theguardian.com/commentisfree/2018/aug/25/ skim-reading-new-normal-maryanne-wolf.

book, and reading through the Bible, your child is gaining less experience and knowledge in key areas that may impact what you have crafted for them in your parenting blueprint.

THE DANGERS

While I've highlighted the rapid changes happening in our digital world, I need to take it a step further and highlight what this means for your child. These changes have certainly brought some benefits (access to information, the ability connect with loved ones from anywhere, etc.), but a set of new dangers have emerged as well. If you want to stay true to your parenting blueprint, you'll need to understand the implications of these dangers for your family, so you can intentionally limit their harmful effect on both you and your child.

Cognitive Development

Jean Piaget was a Swiss psychologist who researched how our brain develops from birth to adulthood. This study of how our brains grow and mature over time is known as cognitive development. His theory has provided a framework for how we expect children to develop at each of four distinct stages.

Recently a new generation of researchers has been working to answer how screen time affects this overall developmental process. One such research effort is the Adolescent Brain Cognitive Development (ABCD) study, which is, "the largest long-term study of brain development and child health in the United States."[6] While its focus is not exclusively on technology and screen time, it is one of the topics the team is continuing to analyze. Studies like this one will help us gain a better understanding of how these cultural shifts affect the brains of current and upcoming generations.

---

6   Adolescent Brain Cognitive Development Study. "About the Study," Accessed January 28, 2023. https://abcdstudy.org/about/.

A 2022 study[7] sought to analyze some of the early published studies from the ABCD by conducting brain scans of three-to-five-year-olds according to their digital media use. Just as was seen in earlier analysis of the ABCD data, the authors found that there were physical effects on the brain from digital media use. Cortical thickness (CT) and sulcal depth (SD) had been reduced. They found:

> accelerated maturation in certain basic areas, such as visual processing, but under-development in other higher-order areas that support more complex skills. Specifically, lower CT and SD have been linked to language development, reading skills and social skills such as complex memory encoding, empathy, and understanding facial and emotional expressions.[8]

With studies like these, we are no longer blind to screen time's physical effects on the brain's cognitive development. The data suggests that this is especially pronounced in younger children, due to the extensive brain development that happens from birth to age five.

In seeking to understand these effects, a group of researchers from Japan followed nearly 60,000 children from their first year through their fourth year of life. Through this extensive cohort study, it was found that, "increased screen time in early childhood was negatively associated with poor performance on developmental screeners."[9] The study was

---

7   John S. Hutton et al., "Associations between Digital Media Use and Brain Surface Structural Measures in Preschool-Aged Children," *Scientific Reports* 12, no. 19095 (2022). doi:10.1038/s41598-022-20922-0.

8   John S. Hutton, "Screen Usage Linked to Differences in Brain Structure in Young Children," *Cincinnati Children's Research Horizon* (blog), November 9, 2022, https://scienceblog.cincinnatichildrens.org/screen-usage-linked-to-differences-in-brain-structure-in-young-children/.

9   Midori Yamamoto et al., "Screen Time and Developmental Performance Among Children at 1-3 Years of Age in the Japan Environment and Children's Study," *JAMA Pediatrics* (September 2023). doi:10.1001/jamapediatrics.2023.3643.

able to clearly demonstrate the correlation between screen time at ages one and two with lower developmental scores at ages two and three. The study concluded by recommending "tailored media plans for each family for the better development of their child."

In addition to these findings, there are also studies that suggest that there is a link between screen time and attention span. Dr. Michael Manos from the Cleveland Clinic states that "Kids aged five or younger who experience two or more hours of daily screen time are nearly eight times more likely to be diagnosed with focus-related conditions, including attention deficit hyperactivity disorder."[10] These findings are supported by multiple studies around the globe that state that there is a link between screen time and your child's ability to focus their attention. Take time to review those *wants* in your blueprint and see what could be affected by limiting a child's ability to focus.

Physical Health

As we've traded bikes and basketballs for video games and YouTube, it isn't surprising that we need to take a serious look at our physical health. However, the connection between the two goes deeper than you may think.

First, there is a multi-faceted connection between screen time and obesity. One collection of experts states that "obesity is one of the best-documented outcomes of screen media exposure."[11] These findings predate the smartphone age, as researchers even correlated increased television viewing with obesity back in the 1980s. Multiple studies have shown that there is a correlation between the amount of screen

---

10 Sara Novak, "Investigating Screen Time's Impact on the Attention Span," *Discover Magazine*, December 10, 2021, https://www.discovermagazine.com/mind/investigating-screen-times-impact-on-the-attention-span.

11 Thomas N. Robinson et al., "Screen Media Exposure and Obesity in Children and Adolescents," *Pediatrics* 140, no. S2 (November 2017): S97–S101. doi:10.1542/peds.2016-1758K.

time consumed and poor nutritional behavior. It's much easier to grab some candy and chips while playing video games than it is to prepare fresh fruit and vegetables.

As I alluded to earlier, one of the biggest areas of concern has to do with sleep. In recent years studies have highlighted a link between increased screen time and reduced sleep duration and quality.[12] In addition, there are more than a few studies that prove that the reduction of sleep quality is making the obesity issue even worse.

Our bodies are greatly affected by light. We take natural cues that help our bodies know when we should be awake and when we should start heading to bed. Our screen-based devices give off multiple colors of light, including blue light, which our bodies associate with the daytime. Using screen-based devices before bedtime has been shown to stop our bodies from releasing natural hormones (such as melatonin) that prepare us for sleep.[13]

Study outcomes like these ultimately led to phone manufacturers creating software-based solutions to reduce blue light exposure in the hours before bed. On Apple devices this feature is called Night Shift, while on Android it is called Night Light. These features don't eliminate all of the blue light, but they do reduce your exposure. If you've ever noticed that your phone has a yellow tint to it near bedtime, this is why.

While the blue light issue may be mitigated partly by the software on our phones, it doesn't change the mental stimulation that occurs when we engage our brains in the moments before trying to fall asleep. If I get a critical email and read it before bed, I can pretty much guarantee it will take me another half hour before I can shut my brain off. Try as we

---

12 Konstantinos D. Tambalis et al., "Insufficient Sleep Duration Is Sleep Duration Is Associated with Dietary Habits, Screen Time, and Obesity in Children," *Journal of Clinical Sleep Medicine* 14, no. 10 (October 2018): 1689–1696. doi:10.5664/jcsm.7374.

13 Nikita A. Wong and Hamed Bahmani, "A Review of the Current State of Research on Artificial Blue Light Safety as It Applies to Digital Devices," *Heliyon* 8, no. 8 (August 2022): e10282. doi:10.1016/j.heliyon.2022.e10282.

might, our brains cannot be turned on and off with the flick of a switch.

Due to these and other factors, increased screen time leads to a longer amount of time required to fall asleep, less overall sleep, and decreased quality of sleep.[14] While this can be a problem for adults, this can be downright dangerous for young, developing brains.

Spiritual Development

Today's young people are facing a tsunami of resistance when it comes to spiritual health and development. First, we can see that they spend the majority of their time being discipled by shallow entertainment. Second, their ability to seek God through prayer is limited as they deal with the effects of screen time on their ability to focus. Third, with a reduced ability to read and comprehend complex texts, the Bible seems unapproachable and incomprehensible to many of them. All these things should be alarming for parents who want to raise their child to be a follower of Jesus.

I am not painting a fatalistic picture here. I believe God is doing powerful things in today's young people. I have seen it myself with the student ministry at my church. My point is that we cannot hold the naive position that there are no direct consequences to excessive screen time for today's youth, even if they do not encounter pornographic, violent, or abusive content online. There is just too much data that proves otherwise.

A world in which we are continually occupied by micro-entertainment and constant distractions at every step, is a world in which we are less able to "Be still, and know that I am God" (Psalm 46:10). Christian writer Ronald Rolheiser puts it this way:

---

14 Matthew A. Christensen et al., "Direct Measurements of Smartphone Screen-Time: Relationships with Demographics and Sleep," *PLOS One* 11, no. 11 (2016): e0165331. doi:10.1371/journal.pone.0165331.

Today, a number of historical circumstances are blindly flowing together and accidentally conspiring to produce a climate within which it is difficult not just to think about God or to pray, but simply to have any interior depth whatsoever . . . We, for every kind of reason, good and bad, are distracting ourselves into spiritual oblivion.[15]

By allowing the spiritual ears of today's youth to be dulled by these distractions, they have been set up to be even more vulnerable to the power of sin in our world. If you want your child to leave spiritual infancy, I strongly recommend that you limit their screen time. If you want to set a proper example for your child, and if you want to have a growing relationship with God yourself, then I recommend you limit your own screen time as well.

No Downtime

Without any limits or boundaries, screen time begins to encroach on every waking moment of every day. While there are profound consequences for this reality that will be covered elsewhere in this book, I want to focus on one by-product of this mentality: screen time while driving.

In 2019 alone, 3,142 people were killed in the United States by distracted driving, and another 424,000 were injured in these accidents.[16] These statistics cover all distracted driver accidents, not just the ones that were caused by using a mobile device while driving. It is notoriously difficult to get an accurate percentage of how many of these can be contributed to mobile devices, as few people want to own up to the true cause of these accidents.

So, how big of an issue is distracted driving? In a recent US study by

---

15 Ronald Rolheiser, *The Holy Longing: The Search for a Christian Spirituality* (New York: Doubleday, 1999), 31–33.

16 National Center for Statistics and Analysis, "Distracted Driving 2019," National Highway Traffic Safety Administration, April 2021. https://crashstats.nhtsa.dot.gov/Api/Public/ViewPublication/813111.

the Insurance Institute for Highway Safety (IIHS) it was found that over one fifth of those surveyed reported engaging in a "modern device distraction" in the thirty days prior to the survey.[17] This includes tasks like making video calls, reading emails, sending text messages, and scrolling social media. While everyone seems to know this behavior is dangerous, the siren call of screen time seems to be too compelling to quell.

I realize that for many of you with a younger child this may seem like a distant concern, but I want to encourage you to consider another perspective. How many times in the past year have you silently supported this dangerous behavior by demonstrating it to your child? Your first step in teaching your child to drive safely is demonstrating the correct behavior in the decade before they ever touch a steering wheel. Your child needs to know that there are times and places where they simply cannot scratch that screen time itch.

Amplification

Each step in *The 7 Essential Steps of Digital Parenting* covers a different topic. Just as I've done with this step, I'll be presenting dangers in the other steps as well. Topics like mental health, explicit content, and even Internet safety all bring their own dangers that we will need to walk through together. So why am I mentioning them here?

If social media is leading to depression or anxiety, more screen time makes it worse. If your child interacts online with other humans, more screen time means more opportunities for a predator to take advantage of the situation. If your child has stumbled onto pornography, more screen time means a greater temptation and more opportunities to fall into sin.

We lay a foundation for all of the other steps by becoming aware of our screen time, limiting it, and using it wisely.

---

17 Aimee E. Cox. et al., "Prevalence of distracted driving by driver characteristics in the United States," *Journal of Safety Research* 86, (2023), 346–356. doi:10.1016/j.jsr.2023.07.013.

HOW MUCH IS ENOUGH?

In 2016 there was a recognition from the American Academy of Pediatrics (AAP) that this massive shift in how children spend their time was not just a neutral change but rather a full-blown health crisis that required formal recommendations for both medical professionals and families. They stated that "multiple developmental and health concerns continue to exist for young children using all forms of digital media to excess."[18] This realization led to a policy statement in their official journal in November 2016, which was reaffirmed in 2022.

This policy statement played a key role in highlighting the dangers of screen time for young children. They stated, "(it) . . . addresses the influence of media on the health and development of children from 0 to 5 years of age, a time of critical brain development, building secure relationships, and establishing health behaviors." Part of this policy statement provided recommendations for parents. A majority of these recommendations focused on limiting the amount and type of screen-based content that children consumed between the ages of 0 and 5.

Age Range	Recommended Amount	Notes
0-18 months	No screen time	Exception for video chatting with family
18-24 months	Limited use	No solo screen time, only high-quality content
2-5 years	1 hour per day	Co-viewing with your child, only high-quality content

Figure 2: AAP recommended screen time for children from birth to age 5[19]

---

18   David Hill et al., "Media and Young Minds," *Pediatrics* 138, no. 5 (November 2016): e20162591. doi:10.1542/peds.2016-2591.

19   Hill et al., "Media and Young Minds," e20162591.

While I think these recommendations are important, I don't think they are comprehensive enough for families looking to protect their child from the dangers we have discussed. They do, however, provide a baseline for screen time limits as well as highlight that not all screen time is equal.

Types of Screen Time

When most parents talk about screen time limits, they are talking about *recreational screen time*. This is when a child decides to watch a show, play a video game, or interact on social media. Since we know that some harmful effects of screen time can occur even if the child is using digital devices for educational purposes, it is essential to have an overall limit that the child cannot exceed. This number should be put into place to make sure that your child is spending a good amount of time away from screens and engaging in physical activity, direct social interactions, and creative outlets. I refer to this number as *total screen time*.

Total screen time is the maximum time your child can be in front of any screen on any given day. This isn't a number your child can increase with good behavior. This isn't a number that can be negotiated. *Any time spent in front of a screen counts toward total screen time.*

When it comes to determining which activities fall into the recreational screen time bucket, consider the following guidelines:

- All screen time counts toward the total screen time limit.

- Any screen time your child does solo that isn't explicitly required (by you, school, or an employer) is recreational screen time.

- Activities that are explicitly required for school or a job do not count toward the recreational screen time limit.

- Any time spent consuming screen time with a parent or guardian does not count toward recreational screen time.

Recommended Limits

Putting the total screen time and recreational screen time numbers together is a key aspect of designing your *Family Screen Time Plan*, which you will be creating as part of the Action Plan for this chapter. While you ultimately will have to decide on these numbers for your own family, I want to provide you with a starting point. The table below includes the recommendations for daily screen time limits from DigitalParenting.com, which are based on the research mentioned in this chapter. You'll notice that in some areas our recommendations are lower than the AAP recommendations.

Age Range	Total Screen Time (hours/day)	Recreational Screen Time (hours/day)	Notes
0–18 months	0	0	*Avoid all screens*
18–24 months	0.5	0	*Parent/child co-viewing, no solo screen activities*
2–5 years	1	0	*Parent/child co-viewing, no solo screen activities*
6–8 years	2	0.5	
9–11 years	3	0.75	
12–14 years	3.5	1	
15–18 years	4	1	

Figure 3: DigitalParenting.com recommended daily screen time limits by age range

If you believe the numbers should be lower for your child, follow your gut. If you believe the numbers should be higher, pray about it. While every family and situation is different, the standard God sets for us as followers of Christ is the same. By setting limits and thoughtfully discussing them with your child, you are setting the foundation for a rich and varied life as well as for self-control when it comes to screen time. Don't forget to review your parenting blueprint as you determine these limits.

I realize that I haven't covered every question related to screen time here. I want to have an ongoing conversation with you through the *Digital Parenting Community*. If you have a question, concern, or challenge while implementing your *Family Screen Time Plan*, please let us know and we will respond.

Use Case

While these limits may seem straightforward, implementing them in real life may prove challenging. To give you an example, I want to walk you through how things work at the Tucker home. This example will help illustrate some important points about screen time limits.

My wife Shannon, a formally educated teacher, homeschools all three of our children: Kaden, Keegan, and Brenna. During the school year, our children regularly engage in learning activities that span both online and classroom education. We estimate that our children consume two hours or less of screen time each school day on educational activities. Since our children currently fit into the 12–14 age range, this is still well within the total screen time of 3.5 hours.

We have decided to forego recreational screen time on school days. As a family, we may still watch something on the TV in the evenings. While we are not regular watchers of traditional television or streaming services, we occasionally watch videos from YouTube channels like *Mark Rober* or *Dude Perfect*. This generally will not exceed 30 minutes, and we will watch it together. This brings the total screen time for an average school day up to 2.5 hours. Even though we could add more, we feel that this is an appropriate level for our children.

On the weekends, we add in recreational screen time. We make it clear that this time is not guaranteed. This time can be taken away. There are also times when we don't have time for it, due to other activities. On a normal weekend, our children can each have an hour of screen time spread across Friday evening, Saturday, and Sunday.

You may be wondering why we settled on an hour for the whole weekend when their recreational screen time could be an hour per child each day. The reason for us is that our children generally watch each other's screen time. When Kaden plays a game on the Nintendo Switch, you can bet that Keegan and Brenna are sitting on the couch, watching his efforts. If our children spread out their recreational time across the whole weekend, they will each do twenty minutes per day, which equals an hour total on each weekend day. This makes Friday the only day of the week on which we hit that total screen time limit.

This leaves some extra time on the weekend when we can inject some other family activities. This could include a movie, a screen-based family game, or a sporting event. There are also plenty of weekends when we don't use any screen time, and instead fill our schedule with other activities that focus on creativity, physical activity, and nature.

ACTION PLAN
Online Resources: https://dp.run/step1

To counteract the inherent dangers of excessive screen time, you'll need to have an Action Plan. However, before we get to what you need to do, I want to define the goal that we are working toward.

Goal: To lead every family member to make wise and healthy decisions regarding the amount and type of screen time they consume.

There are a few pieces of this goal we need to unpack. First, you will notice that this isn't just a goal for your child. This goal includes *you*. It is impossible for anyone to disciple their child effectively if their face is continually buried in their phones. If you want a gut punch, ask your child if they wish you used your phone less. Data suggests that our inability to provide our children with an undistracted version of ourselves may lead to mental health challenges in their preteen and teen years.[20] Look up and set your phone down.

Second, you will notice that this goal doesn't say to just put a tool in place to turn off the Internet at specific times in your home. I hope you recognize that at some point your child will have to make their own decisions about screen time. We need to create a foundation that will enable them to learn how to implement healthy habits as they transition from their teen years into adulthood. This cannot be accomplished with an app, a hack, or a quick-fix parenting technique. It will take ownership on your part and intentional conversations with your child.

If you are ready to dive in and get a handle on the screen time in your family, we've finally arrived at the steps you need to take. Don't forget to mark off these items on your Action Plan Tracker once you complete them.

1. CREATE A FAMILY SCREEN TIME PLAN
FOR ALL FAMILIES

It may surprise you, but the first task for addressing screen time in your family is to audit your own behavior. You cannot expect your child to adopt habits that are the opposite of what you model for them daily. If you cannot put your own phone down, or if you are attempting to reply to emails while you are watching a movie as a family, you can expect that they will adopt those same habits.

I realize that for some of you, this may seem challenging. Depending on your job, you may feel that you need to be constantly reachable by colleagues, clients, or customers. It is important to remember that this has a cost. Being constantly distracted, never fully present, and always working will seem normal to your child. You may be giving them a silent endorsement for these habits without even realizing it.

---

20 Xiaochun Xie and Julan Xie, "Parental Phubbing Accelerates Depression in Late Childhood and Adolescence: A Two-Path Model," *Journal of Adolescence* 78 (2020): 43–52. doi:10.1016/j. adolescence.2019.12.004.

Because of this, the first part of the *Family Screen Time Plan* is just for the parents and guardians. Your child doesn't ever need to see this part. This is where you set expectations on how you will use your devices when you are at home. It is essential that you take a hard look at your own device usage before answering the questions in this section.

Once you have analyzed your own device usage, you will be ready to move to the next step. If someone else is involved in the parenting process, I suggest you meet with them and answer these questions together:

- When will you abstain from device usage altogether?

- What family activities will be device free?

- When will you regularly set aside time to meet with your spouse/ co-parent and discuss the plan?

The second part of the Family Screen Time Plan is for your child, and they should see this posted somewhere prominently in your home. This plan will answer four questions that govern how your child may consume screen time in your home:

- Which devices can be used?

- Where can devices be used?

- When can devices be used?

- What are the total and recreational screen time limits for each child?

Once you have completed the Family Screen Time Plan, you'll need to implement it. This includes both the parent and child sections. There may be a temptation to delay this step, but once this plan is completed, it needs to be implemented within a week. After you've implemented it, there may be a need to make some adjustments. Just be sure that you and your spouse are both on board with the changes and that you have clearly communicated these changes to your child.

*The template for a **Family Screen Time Plan** is available in the online resources for this chapter, along with a guide on how to audit your device usage.*

2. PUT SOFTWARE LIMITS IN PLACE WHERE POSSIBLE
FOR FAMILIES WITH CHILDREN CURRENTLY USING DEVICES

There is one additional protection that can greatly help you implement your Family Screen Time Plan. Many devices have support for time limits and curfews built in. You cannot rely on these to fully implement your plan, but these settings can help enforce whatever rules you've put in place.

I've talked with multiple parents who have had kids wake up in the middle of the night, sneak a tablet into their room, and get some extra gaming or social media time in. We can remove this temptation entirely by making sure that access to those devices and the Internet is unavailable when they should be sleeping. Software can't implement the plan for you, but it can absolutely support it.

Identify the devices your child has access to in the home. Determine which ones will have limits or curfews put into place. Review the resources at DigitalParenting.com to help you implement these changes. We regularly update the resources there to ensure you have the most up-to-date information to implement these parameters.

We provide instructions for setup on common devices in the online resources for this step.

3. TEACH YOUR CHILD BIBLICAL CONCEPTS ABOUT TIME
FOR FAMILIES WITH CHILDREN AGES 7+

If you want your child to become a committed and obedient follower of Jesus, you need to equip them to handle the spiritual challenges they will face. By leading your family through the included Bible study, you can teach your child how to follow God's instructions for how we use our time. This will equip them with tools they can use to determine whether something is a wise or unwise use of their time.

These Bible studies are designed to be completed as a family. There are elements that you can adjust in the study, based on your child's age. If your child isn't yet seven, you can store this activity away until later. If you choose to do so, however, make a note in the tracker for when you plan to cover it.

Each of the Bible studies included in the online resources was created to be easy to teach, even if you haven't ever led your child in a Bible study before. With thirty minutes of prep time or less, you can be ready to lead your child through this material.

This Bible study guide is available in the online resources for this chapter.

6

STEP 2

Avoiding Inappropriate Content

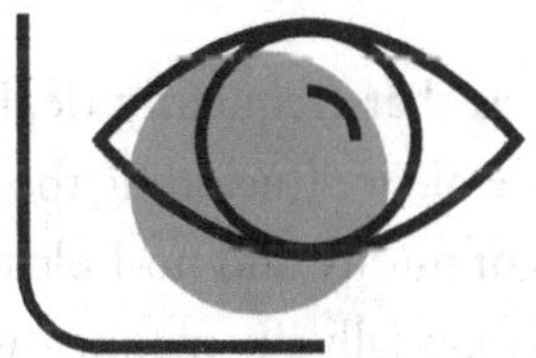

The eye is the lamp of the body. So, if your eye is healthy, your whole body will be full of light, but if your eye is bad, your whole body will be full of darkness. If then the light in you is darkness, how great is the darkness! (MATTHEW 6:22–23)

IN THE 1960s Sam Ginsberg owned a convenience store on Long Island, where he kept explicit magazines behind the counter for his customers to purchase. The reason this convenience store has a place in US history is that Sam didn't just sell this content to adults. On a few occasions he allowed a sixteen-year-old boy to purchase the magazines as well.

The resulting legal case around this action made it all the way to the Supreme Court of the United States. The Supreme Court sided with the original New York state law, which defined this material as "harmful to minors."[1] On April 22, 1968 the entire legal system sought to enforce laws to protect young people from inappropriate content.

If we fast-forward to 2011, the world was introduced to *Game of Thrones* on HBO and its newly launched streaming service, HBO Go. Over its eight seasons, it pulled in an average of 18.6 million viewers per episode and nabbed 59 Emmy Awards.[2] While the show was geared for adults, the degree to which it pushed the bounds for sexual content, violence, and language cannot be overstated. Common Sense Media described the series as a:

> big-budget fantasy series that frequently depicts brutal battles and graphic, detailed acts of violence (including those against children and women), as well as lots of nudity and no-holds-barred sexuality. The latter is portrayed in an especially iffy manner, with explicit discussion and depiction of incest, adultery, and rape.[3]

Given the explicit nature of this content, what societal protections existed when this show was launched on the world? The types of content that were once hidden away behind the counter of a convenience store are now ever-present in our homes via the magic of the Internet. All the responsibility for keeping this content away from your child now rests on your shoulders. It's a tremendous responsibility. If you feel inadequate for this task, you are not alone.

---

1   Ginsberg v. New York, 390 U.S. 629 (1968).

2   "'Game of Thrones' Draws 7.1 Million Viewers for Blood-Filled Finale," Reuters, June 16, 2014, https://www.reuters.com/article/us-television-gameofthrones-idUSKBN0ER2N520140616.

3   Matt Springer, "Game of Thrones," *Common Sense Media*, Accessed October 23, 2023, http://www.commonsensemedia.org/tv-reviews/game-of-thrones.

A DEFINITION

Inappropriate content takes many forms—from the pornographic, violent, and suggestive to the perverse. While this content existed long before tablets and smartphones did, I'll be focusing on what gets consumed digitally. Throughout this book, the working definition I will use is:

> **Inappropriate Content**: *Any digital content that goes against God's standards.*

I realize that this definition can create some gray areas. Every type of content exists on a spectrum. While some types of content, such as pornography, are clearly against God's standards for us, other types of content aren't as clear. Before we start examining the types of content that exist online, we should take a step back and review God's standards from the Bible. The text has a lot to say about what we let into our minds.

THE BIBLICAL STANDARD

The phrase *you are what you eat* has been around for a century and a half. While there is some truth to this phrase in the physical world, the Bible says *you are what you watch* in the spiritual world. At the beginning of this chapter, I included a passage from the book of Matthew. I don't want you to miss the significance of these verses. Let's revisit the words Jesus shared as a part of the Sermon on the Mount:

> The eye is the lamp of the body. So, if your eye is healthy, your whole body will be full of light, but if your eye is bad, your whole body will be full of darkness. If then the light in you is darkness, how great is the darkness! (Matthew 6:22–23)

If we believe Jesus's words, we must accept that what we watch affects us. Jesus doesn't give any qualifications here, so we can rightly assume that this applies to all of us—young and old, new and mature believers, men and women. It is true, irrespective of our age or level of maturity.

Every explicit online video, violent video game, suggestive image, and inappropriate meme has an effect on us spiritually. How then do we live in a culture where we cannot fully escape this type of content?

I have included a list of biblical principles that have helped our family navigate this challenge. While this list isn't exhaustive, it provides a foundation for evaluating various types of content as well as choosing our response to it.

WE ARE CALLED TO GLORIFY GOD IN ALL WE DO.

While we might not generally consider our online activity as something that glorifies God, Paul says that we should. He instructs the church in Corinth, "So, whether you eat or drink, or whatever you do, do all to the glory of God" (1 Corinthians 10:31).

WE VALUE EVERY HUMAN BEING, SINCE WE ARE ALL CREATED IN THE IMAGE OF GOD.

When we study the very first chapter of the Bible, we gain insight into God's view of creation: "Then God said, 'Let us make man in our image, after our likeness'" (Genesis 1:26a). The concept of God's image residing in all humans should lead us to honor all people. Because all of us are made in God's image, we view all people we encounter not as objects of our entertainment but as people worthy of respect. We should therefore not consume content that degrades or devalues other human beings.

WE SHOULD NOT LOOK AT ANOTHER PERSON IN LUST.

Jesus himself spoke of the dangers of lust during His Sermon on the Mount. "But I say to you that everyone who looks at a woman with lustful intent has already committed adultery with her in his heart"

(Matthew 5:28). This phrase gives us a stern warning about how we look at other people outside of the bond of marriage.

But if you stop reading at this verse in Matthew 5, you'll have missed the magnitude of what Jesus was trying to convey. He was dead serious about lust: "If your right eye causes you to sin, tear it out and throw it away. For it is better that you lose one of your members than that your whole body be thrown into hell" (Matthew 5:29). We could unpack a lot with this verse, but what I want you to understand is the level of spiritual danger Jesus expresses here about lustful intent: It is not innocent. It is not safe. It does have victims and it does have consequences.

WE ARE CALLED TO FOCUS ON THINGS THAT ARE PRAISEWORTHY.

Have you ever stopped to evaluate what captivates your mind? Some things tend to dominate our thoughts and propel us into action. Other thoughts can cause us to freeze in fear or shame. Paul provides an entire list of things we should focus on in his letter to the church at Philippi:

Finally, brothers, whatever is true, whatever is honorable, whatever is just, whatever is pure, whatever is lovely, whatever is commendable, if there is any excellence, if there is anything worthy of praise, think about these things. (Philippians 4:8)

WE ARE CALLED TO AVOID TALK THAT IS CORRUPTING OR UNWHOLESOME.

Paul gave instructions to the church at Ephesus, stating that they should, "Let no corrupting talk come out of your mouths, but only such as is good for building up, as fits the occasion, that it may give grace to those who hear" (Ephesians 4:29). I realize that defining specific words and types of conversations that fall into the corrupting category can be challenging. Instead of simply categorizing good words and bad words, let's strive instead to evaluate whether our talk brings grace to those who hear it.

These principles provide a foundation for evaluating content. The Bible clearly says a great deal more, but these principles can help guide us as we encounter the various types of content that exist within our culture. Later in this chapter I'll be explaining how we have chosen to implement these principles within our home.

WHAT'S OUT THERE

I recently had the opportunity to pick up someone at the airport who had never stepped foot in the United States before. This individual was starting a doctoral program at the University of Tennessee, and he had never been outside the Asian country he called home. Our car ride from the airport was filled with all sorts of questions about why things are the way they are here in Tennessee.

Similarly, I realize that some of you do not understand the media-driven world in which today's youth exist. My goal is to provide you with the knowledge that will help you navigate a world that may seem completely foreign to you. I'll try to explain how the culture has gotten here and which real temptations your child may face every day.

Pornography

Pornography has changed a great deal since the days of Sam Ginsberg's convenience store. It is notoriously difficult to put numbers on the size of the pornography industry, but in 2015 multiple researchers have valued it between 10 and 12 billion dollars annually in the United States alone.[4] Given the realities of the pandemic years, I wouldn't be surprised if this number has more than doubled since.

The types of available content have also greatly shifted since the early

---

4   "Things Are Looking Up in America's Porn Industry," *NBC News*, January 20, 2015, http://www.nbcnews.com/business/business-news/things-are-looking-americas-porn-industry-n289431.

days of the industry. Just as drug users require ever increasing doses to achieve the same high, pornography viewers often seek content that pushes the limits more and more to achieve the same level of satisfaction. This means that with very little effort, your child can come across content that depicts any sexual experience the human mind can conceive.

To gain participants for the creation of these explicit photos and videos, many porn-producing enterprises have resorted to human trafficking and rape. I realize that this sounds like an overstatement of the facts, but simply taking time to review the associated lawsuits and survivor stories will prove that, if anything, I am understating the reality. One recent example comes from the anti-porn resource site, FightTheNewDrug.org:

> In 2019, a porn company called "GirlsDoPorn" was charged with sex trafficking almost two dozen women in a giant scheme out of San Diego. A few months later, earlier in 2020, 22 Jane Does won a lawsuit against the company for forcing, tricking, and coercing them into shooting porn. They had been operating since 2015 and allegedly trafficked and exploited many more women than those who participated in the lawsuit.[5]

You might think that the content they produced was buried in some back corner of the dark web, but you'd be wrong. The content was posted to the 12th most popular site on the Internet: Pornhub.

Sexting

I grew up as a part of the "true love waits" church generation. In many ways, this was a reaction to a lack of discussions about sex among previous generations. We were often reminded that premarital sex could

---

5   "How to Tell if Someone in a Porn Video is a Trafficking Victim," Fight the New Drug, Accessed February 20, 2023, https://fightthenewdrug.org/how-can-you-identify-sex-trafficking-victims-in-porn/.

lead to pregnancy and sexually transmitted diseases. Today's youth have figured out a way to completely avoid these concerns: sexting.

> **Sexting**: Sending explicit images, videos, or messages to another person via a digital device. The individual pieces of explicit content are often referred to as a sext.

The data shows that fewer teens are having sex[6], but a diet of pornography and sexting has replaced in-person physical intimacy. This approach sidesteps the traditional risks of pregnancy and disease while also opening the door to someone in another city, state, or country. For many, sexting doesn't even need to occur in the context of a relationship.

How prevalent is this behavior? A recent meta-study analyzed thirty-nine different research papers on sexting which analyzed both male and female youth through age 18. By examining their findings, which covered several different countries globally, we can see that 34.8% of those interviewed have received a sext and 19.3% have sent one. Another 14.5% have forwarded sexts that they have received without consent from the one who created the content.[7] With over a third of those surveyed receiving this type of content, this dangerous behavior is far from an anomaly.

User-Generated Pornography

Pornography is no longer limited to a collection of adult film actors. Increasingly the industry is enabling people to produce their own explicit photos and videos. While this is supposed to be limited to users who are eighteen or older, that line is often breached.

As I already mentioned, Pornhub is one of the busiest sites on the

---

6   "2019 Youth Risk Behavior Survey Data," Centers for Disease Control and Prevention, Accessed January 27, 2023, http://www.cdc.gov/healthyyouth/data/yrbs/data.htm.

7   Camille Mori et al., "Are Youth Sexting Rates Still on the Rise? A Meta-analytic Update," *The Journal of Adolescent Health* 70, no. 4 (2022): 531–539. doi:10.1016/j.jadohealth.2021.10.026.

Internet. It also allows users to upload their own pornographic content. One study indicates that Pornhub's monthly traffic is greater than that of such popular sites as Amazon, Netflix, Reddit, or LinkedIn.[8]

Serena Fleites was only thirteen in 2014, when the first video of her found its way onto Pornhub. Her eighth-grade crush asked her to send a naked video, and she agreed. What she didn't know was that these videos, which she continued to send, were being uploaded for the whole world to see. You may be wondering how Pornhub could have known that the girl was underage. Well, in this case, the first video was titled "13-Year Old Brunette Shows Off For the Camera", and it garnered over 400,000 views and an unspecified amount of ad revenue for Pornhub before it was taken down.[9]

In 2021 Serena filed a lawsuit against MindGeek, Pornhub's parent company, the boyfriend, Visa, and a small handful of additional plaintiffs. A judge found that Visa "made the decision to continue to recognize MindGeek as a merchant, despite its alleged knowledge that MindGeek monetized child porn."[10] This became a big enough controversy that Visa and Mastercard both suspended the processing of payments for MindGeek. Sites like Pornhub that allow user-generated content have moved underage porn from the deepest pits of the Internet to some of the most popular sites in the world.

Importantly, even if everyone in the content is of age, that doesn't mean that everyone has consented to having the content posted online

8   "The World's Busiest Websites in 2020," Fasthosts, Accessed February 20, 2023, https://www.fasthosts.co.uk/web-hosting/busiest-websites/data.

9   "Judge Refuses to Dismiss Visa as a Defendant in Suit Against Pornhub for Child Pornography," The Villanova Law Institute to Address Commercial Sexual Exploitation, September 8, 2022, https://cseinstitute.org/judge-refuses-to-dismiss-visa-as-a-defendant-in-suit-against-pornhub-for-child-pornography/.

10   Kate Rooney and Yun Li, "Visa and Mastercard Suspend Payments for Ad Purchases on Pornhub and Mindgeek amid Controversy," *CNBC*, August 4, 2022. http://www.cnbc.com/2022/08/04/visa-suspends-card-payments-for-ad-purchases-on-pornhub-and-mindgeek-amid-controversy.html.

for the world to see. One type of content that is posted without consent is *revenge porn*. In some relationships, these inappropriate images and videos are used as weapons. In many cases, this content is uploaded for the purpose of harming the other person after the relationship has ended.

Young women in particular are more likely to be targeted: One in 10 women under the age of 30 have experienced threats of nonconsensual image sharing, a much higher rate than either older women or older and younger men.[11]

There is another significant trend luring young people into user-generated pornography: profit. The site OnlyFans is designed for any creator who wants to enable users to subscribe to their content for a monthly fee. While many types of content exist on the platform, it is dominated by pornography. Today's young people have heard stories of some young adult creators on the platform making up to $1 million a day on the platform . . . and for many, it is tempting. Since our culture ignores the moral implications of pornography, this is seen as a savvy business venture rather than a platform of degradation. OnlyFans is projected to hit $2.5 billion in revenue in 2022.[12]

Video Games

Modern video game consoles have powerful capabilities for depicting realistic, violent, explicit, and even profane experiences. This is a far cry from the 8-bit characters of my childhood. With these capabilities comes an increasing ability to present content that goes against God's standards in a way that looks and feels real.

One example of this type of game is *Grand Theft Auto V* from

---

11   Amanda Lenhart, Michele Ybarra, and Myeshia Price-Feeney, "Nonconsensual Image Sharing: One in 25 Americans has been a victim of 'Revenge Porn'," *Data & Society*, December 13, 2016. https://datasociety.net/library/nonconsensual-image-sharing.

12   Dan Primack, "Onlyfans Has Tons of Users, but Can't Find Investors," *Axios*, August 19, 2021. http://www.axios.com/2021/08/19/onlyfans-investors-struggle.

Rockstar Games. This game elicited the following review from Common Sense Media:

> It brims with gang violence, nudity, extremely coarse language, and drug and alcohol abuse. Playing as hardened criminals, players kill not only fellow gangsters but also police officers and innocent civilians using both weapons and vehicles while conducting premeditated crimes, including a particularly disturbing scene involving torture. Women are frequently depicted as sexual objects, with a strip club mini-game allowing players to fondle dancers' bodies, which are nude from the waist up. Players also have the opportunity to make characters use marijuana and drink alcohol, both of which impact their perception of the world.[13]

As of August 2022, it is estimated that this game has been purchased over 170 million times globally.[14] I assume that a vast majority of the parents who have this game in their homes have no idea what it contains. Despite its content, it is currently number two on the list of the best-selling video game of all time.[15]

While on the one hand we have such explicit games that glorify violence, murder, and abuse, many games don't violate the biblical principles we discussed earlier. Some games teach educational concepts in a profound way; some create environments for family fun; and some encourage creativity in ways that were impossible, even just a few years ago. This generation of video games isn't all dark. As a parent, you do

---

13　Chad Sapleha, "Grand Theft Auto V (2022)," *Common Sense Media*, Accessed: March 5, 2023, http://www.commonsensemedia.org/game-reviews/grand-theft-auto-v-2022.

14　"Take-Two Interactive Software, Inc.," Take-Two Interactive Software, November 2022, https://ir.take2games.com/static-files/f0f9ff64-0b90-4781-bd7c-76e016e03a1e.

15　Wikipedia. "List of Best-Selling Video Games," Last modified August 17, 2023. https://en.wikipedia.org/wiki/List_of_best-selling_video_games.

need to be aware of what is out there, though, and do your research before you purchase.

I realize that you may bristle at me including video games in this chapter, but I don't believe that any area of our digital lives is beyond scrutiny. If you embrace the biblical principles I have covered in this chapter, you'll need to take the time to determine which games glorify God and which do not.

There is one additional aspect of gaming that you need to know about: it has become a much less solitary activity than it used to be. Many games include real-time communication with other players. Many platforms allow players to talk with each other as they compete against each other. While this type of communication isn't supported for all games, platforms like Discord enable players to keep that channel of communication open, no matter what they are doing.

While these communication channels can enhance the social aspect of video gaming, the words shared on them are unmonitored. While your child may be playing a game without much objectionable content, they may be playing with someone who is utilizing profane language or sexualized commentary.

Shows & Movies

There was a time when placing your child in front of the TV in the living room came with some assurances. There were words they would not hear, things they would not see, and the worldview contained within the shows wouldn't be too different from your own. Since network television went over government-regulated airwaves, many of these assumptions were baked into the law in the United States.

If we fast-forward to the present day, many things have shifted. While televisions still sit in most living rooms, people are more likely to watch content on other devices. When we do watch content on TV, it is less likely to come from the big broadcast networks. Streaming services like Netflix, Hulu, Amazon Prime Video, and Disney+ are eating up larger and larger chunks of our culture's viewing time. These streaming services are no longer bound by the laws that govern network TV, so traditional expectations of what is acceptable have evaporated almost overnight.

This creative freedom unbound by regulation has led to shows pushing the limits of what is acceptable. The most popular show of all time on Netflix is the Korean drama *Squid Game*. While the show features a hefty amount of sex, bad language, and nudity, it really exceeds expectations with its violence. Slate's review of the show reads:

> This is not a show for viewers who dislike seeing people shot at close range (or stabbed, or killed by falling from a height, and so on). There are literally hundreds of such deaths in the show's nine episodes, with a bonus dissection scene, if what you really crave is to see some intestines. And almost everybody on the show is afraid, all the time—the actors are constantly trembling, crying, and shaking, under the most extreme forms of duress.[16]

During the peak of the show's popularity, I often heard middle schoolers at our church discussing the latest episode. Many of these students are watching the show by themselves, with no one to help them process what they are seeing. Is it any wonder that we are growing callous[17] to the sufferings of other humans when we are consuming content that leverages suffering as entertainment?

THE DANGERS

16　Rebecca Onion, "Netflix's No. 1 Show Will Make You Feel Gross, but You Should Watch It Anyway," *Slate*, September 22, 2021, https://slate.com/culture/2021/09/squid-game-netflix-review.html.

17　Laura Stockdale et al., "Cool, Callous and in Control: Superior Inhibitory Control in Frequent Players of Video Games with Violent Content," *Social Cognitive and Affective Neuroscience* 12, no. 12 (December 2017): 1869–1880. doi:10.1093/scan/nsx115.

God's standards are designed to lead us to a more abundant life,[18] and this includes the things we dwell on and the content we consume. While it may seem like I am advocating for taking away specific types of content, instead I'm advocating for your family to avoid the dangers that come with watching these types of content. Let's take a look at the documented dangers of consuming inappropriate content.

Pornography

Pornography is not new, but its availability has increased by an order of magnitude. This availability has led to studies on the effects of ever-increasing exposure to it. Just as with excessive screen time, studies have shown that extended exposure to pornography physically changes the brain. One 2019 study from the Journal of Psychosexual Health observed that "Pornography can bring about significant changes in the brain similar to what can be seen in drug addictions."[19] This study did not stop there. It began to examine additional effects tied to "excess viewing," including anxiety, depression, sexual dysfunction, lower degrees of social interaction, and higher levels of delinquent behavior among others.

It is mind-boggling that modern societies have the data on the psychological effects of pornography and documented cases of how human trafficking is intimately linked to the industry, and yet refuse to condemn it or create legislation that limits its reach.

Many of you may believe you know what your child has been exposed to, but the data suggests that you may be wrong. One study found that "75% of parents in the survey thought their child hadn't seen pornography online, but in reality 53% of their children reported

---

18 See John 10:10.

19 Manju George et al., "Psychosocial Aspects of Pornography," *Journal of Psychosexual Health* 1, no. 1 (2019): 44–47. doi:10.1177/2631831818821535.

that they had in fact seen it."[20] Even if your kids don't have unrestricted device access, chances are that a neighbor, classmate, or friend at church can browse whatever they want on their phone.

Just a few years ago, one study placed the average age of the first pornography exposure at thirteen.[21] In more recent findings, it was eleven.[22] As I was writing this book, a study in the UK warned that children as young as nine were being exposed to pornography.[23] The secretive nature of this type of exposure makes it tricky to get an accurate age.

In my conversations with parents, I've learned that most families are not addressing this issue early enough. If you don't prepare your child for what they may encounter, they will have to figure it out for themselves. If they choose poorly, it may negatively impact them for the rest of their lives. If you value the mental health of your child, the health of their current and future relationships, their relationship with you as their parent, and ultimately their relationship with God, I plead with you to not ignore the dangers of pornography.

Sexting

Sexting presents its own set of risks. Very often the images and videos shared when sexting do not remain private. Some apps like Snapchat provide the promise of self-deleting messages. While these apps limit the ways in which someone can download and save the images you send

---

20 "Young People, Pornography & Age-Verification," British Board of Film Classification, 2020, http://www.bbfc.co.uk/about-classification/research.

21 "Age of First Exposure to Pornography Shapes Men's Attitudes Toward Women," American Psychological Association, August 3, 2017, http://www.apa.org/news/press/releases/2017/08/pornography-exposure.

22 Alan McKee, "Yes, Your Child Will Be Exposed to Online Porn. But Don't Panic — Here's What to Do Instead," *The Conversation*, November 16, 2020. https://theconversation.com/yes-your-child-will-be-exposed-to-online-porn-but-dont-panic-heres-what-to-do-instead-149900.

23 Shiona McCallum, "Children as Young as Nine Exposed to Pornography," *BBC News*, January 31, 2023. https://www.bbc.com/news/technology-64451984.

them, they by no means eliminate the possibility. Based on a recent study, 14.5% of surveyed teens have forwarded sexts that they have received without consent from the one who created the content.[24] Once the image or video has been sent, there is no *undo* button.

The biggest danger when it comes to sexting is shame, leading to serious mental health struggles and even suicide. As these private images and videos are shared, they are often spread to classmates at lightning speed. This leaves the one pictured in the media exposed, and far too many young people have taken life-ending actions to avoid facing this shame. A 2012 study found that youth who engage in sexting were 5.27 times more likely to have attempted suicide than their peers.[25]

Sexting can have profound legal consequences too. Let's imagine an underage girl finally agrees to send a nude picture to her underage boyfriend. In this case, sexting is also the distribution of child pornography. If the boyfriend sends the picture to multiple other guys in his school, each of them could be found guilty of possessing child pornography. The girl could be charged with producing child pornography. If convicted, they all would likely have to register as sex offenders, a label that would follow them for the rest of their lives.

This isn't a hypothetical situation. It really happens. I learned this story from an interview I had with a school resource officer back in 2018. These incidents occurred in his school, and he explained to me the difficulty of resolving the situation, due to how far the images had spread. According to him, sexting incidents in middle and high schools have become commonplace.

Several states have changed the laws around sexting in recent years to place these offenses in a separate category from child pornography. Still, in the United States these situations are handled differently from

---

24 Mori et al., "Are Youth Sexting Rates Still on the Rise?"

25 Joseph A. Dake et al., "Prevalence and Correlates of Sexting Behavior in Adolescents," *American Journal of Sexuality Education* 7, no. 1 (2012): 1–15. doi:10.1080/15546128.2012.6509 59.

state to state. Global laws also vary greatly on this topic. There is no safe way to engage in this behavior if the subject is underage. To avoid this danger, youth must avoid sexting completely.

Video Games

While we could talk about many areas of concern in video games, including profane language, drug use, virtual nudity, and hypersexualized experiences, instead I want to focus on just one area: violence. The degree to which you can encounter violence in video games is unique in both realism and frequency.

In our culture, video games are big business, making a revenue of over $130 billion globally, as of 2019.[26] There has been a great deal of effort placed on downplaying any study that shows a negative effect of video gameplay. I'm not surprised that parents are confused about what the data really shows. Thankfully, in recent years there have been meta-studies that have examined the collective research. When examining the data as a whole, there are some serious concerns that emerge, especially regarding games that feature the personalized violence of one human character acting to kill another human character in a game.

> One cannot ignore the comprehensive reviews that indicate violent game play has a significant effect on aggressive behaviour, affect, cognition and empathy across work conducted with over 130,000 participants . . . the effects have consistently been reported as significant findings with various age groups and in a number of different cultural settings.[27]

---

26 Yuji Nakamura, "Peak Video Game? Top Analyst Sees Industry Slumping in 2019," *Bloomberg*, January 23, 2019. http://www.bloomberg.com/news/articles/2019-01-23/peak-video-game-top-analyst-sees-industry-slumping-in-2019.

27 Lavinia McLean and Mark Griffiths, "The Psychological Effects of Video Games on Young People: A Review," *Aloma: Revista de Psicologia, Ciències de l'Educació i de l'Esport* 31, no. 1 (2013), 119–133. http://www.revistaaloma.net/index.php/aloma/article/view/184.

In addition, when Dr. Craig Anderson examined the collective studies on violent video games, he noted several trends that were found in the research with "considerable consistency:"[28]

- **Violent video games affect our thoughts and actions.** The studies show an increase in aggressive behavior, thoughts, and emotions (affect).

- **Violent video gameplay affects our bodies.** The studies demonstrate that our bodies respond strongly during gameplay, as players experience changes in breathing and blood pressure (physiological arousal).

- **Violent video games decrease our desire to engage in helping (prosocial) behaviors.** Engaging in violent video gameplay reduces our empathy for those around us, leading us to do less for those in need around us.

While I believe that violent video games present a real risk to today's youth, I do not think that every child who plays a first-person shooter game will become a murderer. Over the years, some parent groups have overstated the effects of these games beyond what the research can prove. However, I've heard a lot more parents express the opinion that there are no consequences for violent video gameplay at all. The research doesn't support that viewpoint either.

OUR HOME

Since inappropriate content exists on a spectrum, you will have to make decisions about where you will draw the line in your own home. Before you dive in and tackle the Action Plan for this step, I want to give you some insight into how we have made those decisions within our own

---

28 Craig A. Anderson, "Violent Video Games: Myths, Facts, and Unanswered Questions," *Psychological Science Agenda*, October 2003, http://www.apa.org/science/about/psa/2003/10/anderson.

home. I'll cover our specific stance on certain content types as well as our thinking behind each decision we've made. I hope this will inspire you to define your own approach.

WE BELIEVE PORNOGRAPHY IS ALWAYS WRONG.

I don't believe there is a defensible position for any Christian to believe that this type of content is acceptable, given the clarity in the Bible. We set clear expectations that this content is not allowed in the home, whether for children or adults. On our home network, pornographic content is blocked by default for everyone. We take this stance both because of the biblical standard against lust and because we believe each person has value.

WE DON'T ALLOW VIOLENT VIDEO GAMES.

We are not against all types of video games. We do have a Nintendo Switch in our home, and our family regularly engages in a *Mario Kart* race or a tennis game on Nintendo Switch Sports. When my wife and I evaluate a video game, we investigate the rating as well as the information about the type of content contained within the game.

When it comes to violence, we don't want to have any first-person shooter games available in our home. We have chosen to draw the line there. While we allow some adventure games that may include some fighting, we don't want to expose our children to the risks that come with wanton virtual violence toward other people, simply for our entertainment.

WE DON'T WATCH CONTENT THAT REGULARLY USES COURSE LANGUAGE.

I realize that profane words exist within a cultural context, but in the culture our family lives in, there are some words we never want our children to say. Because of this, we don't want to watch content that regularly uses these words. We certainly see some words as worse than others, so we evaluate each movie, show, and video game based on the words it uses. This often means that our family misses out on the popular series of the day, and we're ok with that.

Some sites provide reviews that help us make these distinctions, and we have provided links to a few recommended sites in the online resources for this chapter.

ACTION PLAN
Online Resources: https://dp.run/step2

Given the discipline it will require to not simply go along with the culture of our day, we must have a clearly defined goal. Just as was the case in the last step, this goal includes you:

GOAL: To prevent inappropriate content from deteriorating your family's relationship with God and others.

I don't want to downplay what is at stake here. Please review your parenting blueprint as you explore the dangers associated with inappropriate content. The side effects of this content likely place many of your *wants* at risk. To protect your family, you will need to leverage a combination of discipleship and technical tools.

There are no perfect tools to protect you and your family from all inappropriate content. Every tool I mention in the online resources can be thwarted. This is why the discipleship element is paramount. I urge you to teach your child to pursue God with their whole heart, or else they might only get skilled at learning to avoid the tools you put in place. The tools have improved greatly in the last decade, but they can't be your only strategy.

Don't forget to log your completed tasks in your Action Plan Tracker.

1. CREATE A FAMILY DEVICE PLAN
FOR ALL FAMILIES

I want your home to be a safe place for your child to grow up in, so your first step is to secure the environment you provide them. In the past, a vast majority of initial exposures to pornography happened in the home, but mobile devices have changed the way in which many kids are now exposed to pornography. Because of this, we will have to attack this risk on multiple fronts.

The first way we will address this is by securing all devices you own. I realize that each of you has different levels of technical ability. This can make implementing your plan challenging. This is why we keep the list of resources on DigitalParenting.com up-to-date, so you can follow a step-by-step guide for configuring our recommended tools on popular devices. Securing a device will cover the following:

- Disabling the ability to install new apps

- Configuring which apps can be used

- Filtering the web and media content that can be viewed on the device

I realize that some of you leverage your child for tech support, but this will need to change. Over 75% of surveyed youth in a recent study said that they could access Internet pornography at home without their caregiver knowing.[29] To avoid this, you need to implement some controls your child should never be able to access or change.

---

29 Siobhán Healy-Cullen et al., "Youth Encounters with Internet Pornography: A Survey of Youth, Caregiver, and Educator Perspectives," *Sexuality & Culture* 26, (2022): 491–513. doi:10.1007/s12119-021-09904-y.

There are multiple ways to block content, but the easiest way is to block your child from using a device. If you have a device you have not yet secured, you can remove their access until you can secure it.

I want to add one note here that is critical for parents to understand: If your child has a phone, you cannot limit your protection to only your home network. At any point, they can turn off Wi-Fi and utilize the unrestricted cellular Internet connection. Phones will require an extra level of protection to make sure that both the Wi-Fi and cellular connections are protected from inappropriate content. The Family Device Plan will walk you through this process.

*The template for a **Family Device Plan** is available in the online resources for this chapter, along with recommendations for tools that can filter the types of content available on your devices.*

2. TEACH YOUR CHILD BIBLICAL CONCEPTS ABOUT INAPPROPRIATE CONTENT
FOR FAMILIES WITH CHILDREN AGES 7+

Teaching your child the biblical concepts that have been covered in this chapter is an essential step. By giving them this foundation, they will understand what God is calling them to do when they inevitably encounter inappropriate content. There will come a time when they will have to make these decisions on their own, so you will need to start training them to make biblical choices now.

These Bible studies are designed to be completed as a family. There are elements that you can adjust in the study, based on your child's age. If your child isn't yet seven, you can store this away until later. If you choose to take this approach, be sure to note in the tracker when you plan to cover the topic.

Bible study guides are available in the online resources for this chapter.

3. DISCUSS PORNOGRAPHY AND ITS DANGERS
FOR FAMILIES WITH CHILDREN AGES 7+

Far too many parents stop after putting content filters in place. I hope we can all agree that blocking content on our home network and devices is an important step, but the risks extend far beyond our homes. At some point your child will be around someone who has a device with unrestricted access to the Internet. It is not possible to block every bit of inappropriate content your child may encounter in the real world.

Since you can't block it all, you must develop a new strategy: You can teach your child how to make the right decisions when it comes to inappropriate content. This is most critical when it comes to pornography. You will need to define it in a way that they will understand and teach them how to respond if they do encounter it.

The included discussion guide will require some preparation on your end, but it will give you the age-specific topics that we encourage you to cover with your child. The online resources for this chapter also include additional books and resources that can be helpful for this discussion. Even though it might feel awkward, the most important step is to have the conversation.

Discussion guides are available in the online resources for this chapter.

7

STEP 3

Safeguarding Mental Health

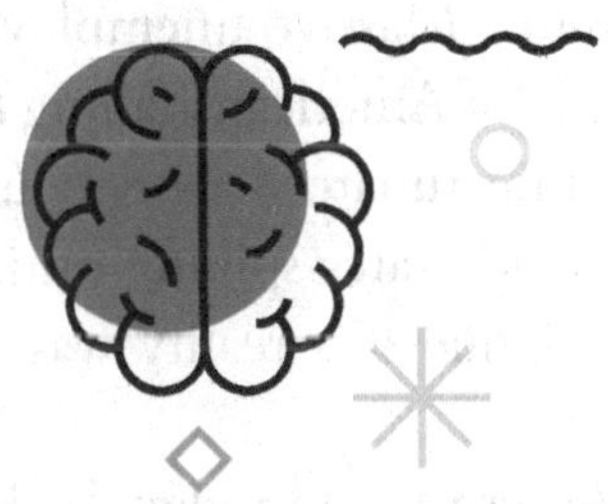

*Peace I leave with you; my peace I give to you. Not as the world gives do
I give to you. Let not your hearts be troubled, neither let them be afraid.*
(JOHN 14:27)

I HAD ARRIVED WELL AFTER MIDNIGHT, so I didn't have the time or
desire to fully take in my surroundings as the yellow New York City
taxi cab dropped me off at my hotel on Water Street. After grabbing
some coffee the next morning, I took off on foot for my 9 a.m. meeting.
I took a right turn down Wall Street and then a left at the George
Washington statue. At this point I was just fifty yards from the massive

stone columns of the New York Stock Exchange Building. This work of neoclassical architecture is a sight to behold.

Before I walk in for my meeting, I pause. I've seen this view before, but not in person. I think back to the black-and-white images of this very building from October 24, 1929. In these photos hundreds of nearby workers from Wall Street were gathered outside grim-faced. The 13% drop in the Dow was the harbinger of the crash that played out over the next seven months. Few realized how bad it would get.

The months that followed were the inflection point that shifted the United States from the roaring twenties into the Great Depression. This period greatly changed everyday life for a vast majority of Americans, including my grandparents. Massive unemployment, banking panics, and an increasing number of Americans falling below the poverty line had taken its toll, and unfortunately many could not find a way out. Historical data shows suicide rates spiking during these early years of the Great Depression.[1] While this reality was unfortunate, it wasn't entirely unexpected.

For much of the Western world today, basic needs are not at risk. While I do realize that there are still far too many people living below the poverty line, the percentages are drastically lower than in the early 1930s. Most people have food, shelter, and employment opportunities. A drive through Chattanooga, Tennessee, will reveal more "Help Wanted" signs than I've ever seen here in the last decade.

Despite this reality, the mental health of middle school, high school, and college students is at risk. Dr. Jean Twenge, psychology professor and author, detailed in her book *Generations* that "Every indicator of mental health and psychological well-being has become more negative among teens and young adults since 2012."[2] In reviewing the data, it

---

1   Feijun Luo et al., "Impact of Business Cycles on US Suicide Rates, 1928–2007," *American Journal of Public Health* 101, no. 6 (2011): 1139–46. doi:/10.2105/AJPH.2010.300010.

2   Jean M. Twenge, *Generations: The Real Differences Between Gen Z, Millennials, Gen X, Boomers, and Silents—and What They Mean for America's Future* (London: Atria Books, 2023), 392.

seems that the period between 2007 and 2012 represents an inflection point for teens and young adults regarding their mental health.

This data is not subtle. It shows that depression among adolescents increased by 52% between 2005 and 2017.[3] There are also increasing trends related to self-harm and suicide. Unlike the Great Depression, there is no major world event to which we can attribute this change. The rapidly deteriorating mental health of today's young people leads us to the question: What happened?

A SOCIAL HISTORY

It may be hard to imagine but in 2003, when I graduated from college, university life existed apart from social media. I was a member of the last college class to graduate before any of the titans of social media were launched upon the world. Mere months after my graduation a new website, Myspace, was launched by Tom Anderson and Chris DeWolfe. This site represented the first of the social media giants that were launched during the first wave of social media.

Between 2003 and 2006 this first wave gave birth to Facebook, Reddit, VK, and Twitter (now known as X). This wave of social media brought concepts like friend lists, the news feed, and social photo sharing to the masses. While it had not yet reached mass popularity, social media was starting to become a part of culture for the under-thirty crowd.

The second wave of social media really began in 2010, with the introduction of Pinterest and Instagram. This was followed immediately by the launches of Snapchat and Twitch in 2011, and Tinder in 2012. These launches changed the way people planned birthday parties, interacted with video games, and even found a potential mate.

This wave also invented the concept of the modern social media

---

3   Jean M. Twenge et al., "Age, Period, and Cohort Trends in Mood Disorder Indicators and Suicide-Related Outcomes in a Nationally Representative Dataset, 2005–2017," *Journal of Abnormal Psychology* 128, (2019):185–99. doi:10.1037/abn0000410.

influencer. Individuals were no longer just following their real-world friends; they were now voraciously consuming content from newly minted online celebrities as well as actors, singers, and even preachers. By the end of 2013, social media use had skyrocketed to 63% among those ages 12 and older in the US.[4]

The third wave really kicked off in 2014 with the launch of Musical.ly. The following year Discord brought voice and video chat to gaming. In this wave, Musical.ly was acquired by ByteDance and merged it with an existing Chinese app, Douyin. The result of this acquisition was the launch of TikTok in 2017.

This wave enabled us to consume even more content from our friends as well as those influencers who continued to gain prominence. As Internet speeds and mobile device capabilities continued to improve, people began to spend more of their time engaging with social media. Short-form content also grew in popularity, which gave rise to the style of media now seen on TikTok, Snapchat, YouTube Shorts, and Instagram Reels. By the end of 2020, the number of adults who actively used social media in the US had risen to 80%.[5] Social media was now firmly rooted in the culture.

THE SIGNS

Throughout this rapid rise of social media, there were signs that something was amiss. The second wave of social media also included research focusing on the connection between its use and mental health. In a 2011 paper from the American Academy of Pediatrics, a new term was coined to demonstrate the potential negative effects of social media:

---

4   "The Infinite Dial 2023," Edison Research, Amazon Music, Wondery, and ART19, March 2023, http://www.edisonresearch.com/infinite-dial-2023-from-edison-research-with-amazon-music-wondery-and-art19/.

5   "The Infinite Dial 2023."

Researchers have proposed a new phenomenon called "Facebook depression," defined as depression that develops when preteens and teens spend a great deal of time on social media sites, such as Facebook, and then begin to exhibit classic symptoms of depression.[6]

Before this point, few people really associated social media use with true depression. While most parents agreed that there could be side effects, they weren't really seen as something that registered on the clinical radar. This initial research and many studies that followed over the next few years changed that perception.

Even at this point, it was only known that social media use was sometimes connected to a decline in mental health. Overall, there was a prevailing belief that social media could only amplify challenges that were preexistent for an individual, such as depression and anxiety.

In 2017 a study led by Dr. Jean Twenge really began to correlate overall screen time use with the mental health decline among teens. According to the study, which examined multiple national surveys in the United States, "adolescents' depressive symptoms, suicide related outcomes, and suicide rates increased between 2010 and 2015, especially among females."[7] At this point, we were jumping beyond observed depression and identifying a link to behavioral concerns, including suicide. While this study was focused on all types of screen time, it was noted that "at least some of the causal arrow points from social media use to mental health issues."

Even as the data began to emerge, many were still skeptical that this shift could be connected to platforms on which people shared pictures

---

6   Gwenn Schurgin O'Keeffe et al., "Council on Communications and Media: The Impact of Social Media on Children, Adolescents, and Families," *Pediatrics* 127, no. 4 (April 2011): 800–804. doi:10.1542/peds.2011-0054.

7   Jean M. Twenge et al., "Increases in Depressive Symptoms, Suicide-Related Outcomes, and Suicide Rates Among U.S. Adolescents After 2010 and Links to Increased New Media Screen Time," *Clinical Psychological Science* 6, no. 1 (2018), 3–17. doi:10.1177/2167702617723376.

of their kids, chronicles of their vacations, and the escapades of their pets. The most convincing evidence was yet to come, however, and it would arrive from a surprising source: Facebook.

The Mic Drop

Fast-forward to 2021. The social media world had evolved. Second and third-wave social media platforms like Instagram, TikTok, and Snapchat were taking up most of the social media market share for the under-twenty crowd. Most of this crowd had fled from Facebook to escape their parents and grandparents. Among this trio, Instagram had the largest monthly active user count, and it was the platform teens were begging their parents to let them join.

On September 14, 2021, the Wall Street Journal reported startling details about Instagram and the potential harm it was causing its users.[8] The most troubling detail from this story was the source of the data: Facebook, the parent company of Instagram.[9] The leaked internal documents painted a very troubling picture of the role social media was playing in unsettling the mental health of a generation.

For three years prior to the publication of the Wall Street Journal article, Facebook was conducting its own studies into the effects of their platforms on its younger users in both the United States and the United Kingdom. The leaked internal documents detailed some of the key findings from these studies, including:[10]

- Among teens who reported suicidal thoughts, 13% of British users and 6% of US users traced the desire to kill themselves to Instagram.

---

8   Georgia Wells et al., "Facebook Knows Instagram Is Toxic for Teen Girls, Company Documents Show," *The Wall Street Journal*, September 14, 2021, http://www.wsj.com/articles/facebook-knows-instagram-is-toxic-for-teen-girls-company-documents-show-11631620739.

9   In late 2021 Facebook reorganized under a new parent company named Meta. Facebook and Instagram now both exist under this parent company.

10   Wells et al., "Facebook Knows Instagram."

- Thirty-two percent of teen girls said that when they felt bad about their bodies, Instagram made them feel worse.

- Teens blame Instagram for increases in the rate of anxiety and depression.

The most disturbing aspect of this story is not the data; it is the fact that Facebook kept this information concealed. At the time, they were moving forward with the plan to make Instagram Kids, which would have enabled preteens to have an account on the platform. Only after a severe public backlash was this plan abandoned and replaced with plans for implementing more extensive parental controls.

Additional Evidence

While the Facebook leak is eye-opening, it is still a single source. Since the release of those internal documents, multiple studies have been published that continue to connect the dots between social media and mental health for preteens, teens, and young adults. I want to highlight two of those studies here.

A collection of European researchers studied over 80,000 participants from the United Kingdom with ages spanning from ten to eighty.[11] From this group more than 17,000 were between the ages of ten and twenty-one. As they examined this younger group, they discovered a direct correlation between increased social media use and a decreased satisfaction in life. This was most evident in girls between the ages of eleven and thirteen and boys between fourteen and fifteen. In addition, this trend was pronounced again at age nineteen for both genders. There was also a finding across all age groups that a decrease in life satisfaction leads to more social media use. So, using social media at certain life stages leads to young people being less satisfied with their lives . . . and

---

11 Amy Orben et al., "Windows of Developmental Sensitivity to Social Media," *Nature Communications* 13, no. 1 (2022): 1649. doi:10.1038/s41467-022-29296-3.

when they are less satisfied with their lives, they turn to social media. This is a vicious cycle that is evident to many of the parents I have spoken with—it also makes the social media platforms a lot of money.

In 2022 a global team of researchers published a paper that examined the observable effects on mental health when social media was introduced on a college campus. When Facebook was initially rolling out, it was only for college students, and it was deployed to a small handful of campuses at a time. This provided a unique opportunity for researchers to compare the existing mental health data from the US college campuses that had Facebook with the ones that did not. After analyzing this data, they discovered that, "College-wide access to Facebook led to an increase in severe depression by 7% and anxiety disorder by 20%."[12] These findings led one of the authors, Dr. Alexey Makarin from the Massachusetts Institute of Technology (MIT), to say:

> When I came to this work, I knew that mental health was an important issue, but to be honest, I thought of it as just one more outcome to study in our social media agenda. When I started to really look into the trends of deteriorating mental health among the young adults, though, I came to realize how truly bad the situation is, and that stuck with me.

It is important to remember that this study focused on a very early version of Facebook, before we had *like* buttons and AI-powered newsfeeds. Unfortunately, it will take years for new studies to emerge that analyze the effect of today's social media. *Technology always moves faster than our ability to understand its effects.*

---

12 Luca Braghieri, Ro'ee Levy, and Alexey Makarin, "Social Media and Mental Health," *SSRN*, July 28, 2022. doi:10.2139/ssrn.3919760.

WHY SOCIAL MEDIA AFFECTS US

Depending upon which generation you were born into, the worst effects of social media may or may not affect you. When we examine the current struggle with social media for teens and young adults, there are several factors that contribute to its net negative effect on their mental health. To help us better understand the challenges that both youth and adults face when using social media, let's review the reasons why it can have such a profound effect on us.

Social Comparison

If you are on social media at all, chances are that you have seen something that made you jealous. Maybe it was someone's new car, a friend's engagement, a beautiful new home for a family member, or even a co-worker's promotion. This jealousy isn't limited to social media—many of us had moments of jealousy long before we could flaunt our life highlights online. But today's social sphere for preteens and teens exists primarily within the walls of social media. The more they scroll through their Instagram feed, the more they are confronted with the greatest highlights from the lives of the friends and celebrities they follow.

This is summed up in an interview with a college student named Emma in Donna Freitas's book, *The Happiness Effect.* "People share the best version of themselves, and we compare that to the worst version of ourselves."[13] All of this can leave us believing that our lives are dramatically falling short of those around us. Emma's story led Freitas to conclude that "Even a beautiful, accomplished young woman from the most prestigious sorority on campus sometimes sees things on social media and starts to feel bad about herself."

---

13 Donna Freitas, *The Happiness Effect* (Oxford: Oxford University Press, 2017), 6.

It's All about the Likes

The decade between our tenth and twentieth birthdays presents a lot of moments for us to put ourselves out there. Asking someone we like to a school dance, presenting in front of a classroom, and even performing a piece of music all require us to accept the fact that some people may like what we offer while others may not. These stress-inducing moments play a role in shaping us for the realities of life.

What if these moments weren't a rare thing? What if multiple times every day our classmates, friends, and even our boyfriend/girlfriend could rate us on who we are? In today's culture, this feedback cycle does indeed exist. Every picture posted to Instagram, every video posted to TikTok, and every snap sent through Snapchat provides an opportunity for those around us to rate not just our content, but also who we are. According to Freitas, "'Likes' take the usual highs and lows of young adult social life and make them quantifiable—a running tally of your self-worth."[14] Even though we all know *likes* have no intrinsic value, preteens, teens, and even adults can fall victim to their allure and become addicted to being noticed.

Fear of Missing Out (FOMO)

In previous generations we had to guess what our friends were doing outside of school. They might return from a weekend of fun, ready to share their escapades with their friends. While there might have been a level of jealousy over not having been invited to come along to these events, that usually passed quickly. This was all before we could see live videos and photos of our friends while they were out, enjoying some exciting adventure while we sat at home, alone.

This reality is known as the *fear of missing out* or the more common acronym, FOMO. Just as with likes, FOMO is another feedback cycle that can cause people to question their relationships or even their

---

14 Freitas, 38.

self-worth. There seems to be a difference between hearing about a party we weren't invited to and seeing a perfectly choreographed TikTok video of the invited partygoers.

There is another side to FOMO as well: Because today's social interactions happen primarily on social media, there is a feeling that they must be continually present online when their friends are posting content. Some social media platforms, like Snapchat, focus on ephemeral content. This type of content appears for a limited period of time only, then disappears. If a friend sends a snap at 2 a.m., you must respond right away, right? If you want to see for yourself how much anxiety this creates, tell a hyper-connected teen that they can't sleep with their phone anymore. FOMO isn't a silly generational behavior. In many cases, it leads to textbook anxiety.

Perfection

I am thankful you all weren't there to see my 9th-grade theater performance of "Seven Brides for Seven Brothers." As far as high school productions go, we did a pretty good job. Do you know who saw it? The people who knew 9th-grade David: my family, friends, teachers, and classmates. It might surprise you, but I don't plan on posting the full version of the musical on LinkedIn for all my professional connections to see.

I realize that this may seem like a silly example, but you need to understand the fact that these dividing lines no longer exist for today's youth. We have seen people lose scholarships, jobs, followers, and influence all because of content that surfaced on social media from their teen years. Since nothing on the Internet can ever truly go away, it has led teens to believe that they need to present perfection all the time. Their online image can affect their friendships, job prospects and—critically important—their college admissions opportunities. Needless to say, this causes an immense amount of stress.

After examining all the conversations she had had with college students at thirteen different campuses across the United States, Donna

Freitas said, "The importance of appearing happy on social media—the *duty* to appear happy—even if you are severely depressed and lonely is so paramount that nearly everyone I spoke to mentioned it at some point."[15] An environment where perfection is valued above reality does not possess the level of vulnerability and safety required to form deep relationships. A generation with increasingly complex mental health challenges is running out of relationships in which they can be real and transparent.

Body Image

In the early 2000s it came to light that a vast majority of the images of models we saw on magazine covers and billboards were heavily manipulated by airbrushing or with digital tools like Adobe Photoshop. As a society, we began to admit that it could be dangerous to promote a standard of beauty that didn't even exist in real life. While the effects of this distortion were problematic even then, social media has amplified this problem beyond celebrities and placed it into the hands of every digitally connected teen.

In 2015 Snapchat launched its lenses feature, which enabled users to modify aspects of their appearance in real time by using filters. These filters ranged from silly to serious, depending on the author's intent. One early Snapchat filter made it seem as though you were puking a rainbow. With this type of filter, there was no risk of blurring the lines between fantasy and reality.

Filters eventually came to most every social media platform. On some platforms like Instagram, people began to use filters—not to create an obviously fake video to send to friends, but to improve aspects of their appearance. Soon a large collection of filters became available that could smooth out blemishes, slim your overall figure, add in some eyelashes, and even make your hair glow.

Just as social comparison plays on our jealousy of possessions and

---

15 Freitas, 15.

experiences, the use of filters amplifies our feelings of inadequacy about our bodies. While the experience is worse for girls, it can also affect boys. How can today's young people possibly compete with a body image that has been perfected by layers of image processing? Another danger exists for the people sharing images that leverage filters. They may wonder: "Will people like the *real* me, or are they only clicking that heart because of the filters I used?"

Comparison, jealousy, and feelings of inadequacy aren't the only consequences of social media's impact on body image. A 2019 Saudi Arabian study found that 48.5% of the female Saudi university students surveyed were "influenced by social media to consider undergoing cosmetic procedures."[16] Now one person's fake representation of themselves is leading to another person's permanent body-altering surgery. Our virtual images are producing real-life consequences. What will they lead to next?

THE DANGERS

Before you can create a plan for dealing with the mental health dangers connected to our digital world, I need you to know what you are up against. While I have alluded to the mental health challenges facing tweens, teens, and young adults, let's dive into them at a deeper level. I pray that by opening your eyes to the severity of this issue, your family will be spared.

Depression & Anxiety

Depression and anxiety are two different conditions, but increasingly psychologists are viewing them as "two faces of one disorder."[17] While

---

16 Khalid Arab et al., "Influence of Social Media on the Decision to Undergo a Cosmetic Procedure," *Plastic and Reconstructive Surgery - Global Open* 7, no. 8 (2019), e2333. doi:10.1097/GOX.0000000000002333.

17 Hara Estroff Marano, "Anxiety and Depression Together," *Psychology Today*, February 5, 2020. http://www.psychologytoday.com/us/articles/200310/anxiety-and-depression-together.

anxiety can present itself as ongoing fear, worry, and panic; depression culminates in a struggle with sadness and hopelessness that negatively affects one's daily life. In many of the studies that examine the connection between youth and social media, these conditions are analyzed together.

I opened this chapter by mentioning that depression among adolescents in the United States increased by 52% between 2005 and 2017.[18] The data used to support this claim comes from the National Survey on Drug Use and Health (NSDUH). This annual survey gathers data on both substance abuse and mental health on both adults and youth from the age of twelve. One of the data points collected is whether those surveyed have had a major depressive episode (MDE) within the last year.

Major Depressive Episode by Gender

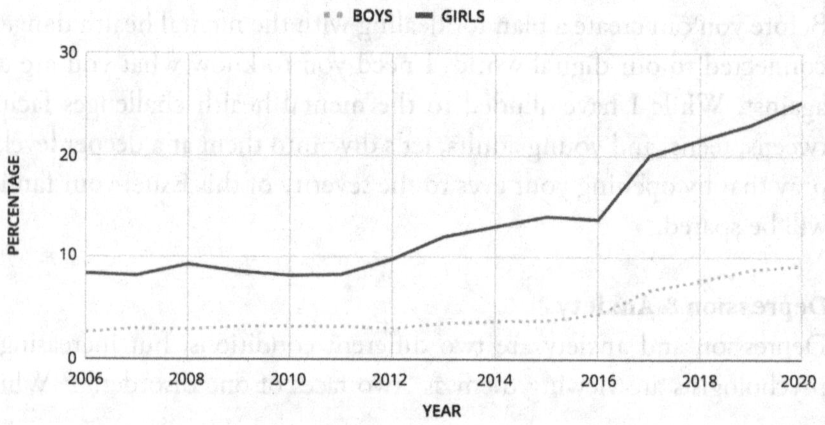

Figure 1 - *Major Depressive Episode by Gender, Data from the National Survey on Drug Use and Health (NSDUH)*

18 Twenge et al., "Age, Period, and Cohort Trends."

When we examine the data, we can see that 2011 serves as a tipping point. Before this, the data was relatively consistent. After this point, the data began to change significantly for girls aged 12-17. Between 2010 and 2020 girls saw a 200% increase in Major Depressive Episodes while boys saw an even larger increase, albeit with much lower values overall.

It may be tempting to assume that this problem is isolated to a specific ethnic, socioeconomic, or geographic segment of this age group, but the research does not support this. The Monitoring the Future (MtF) surveys of 8th, 10th, and 12th graders in the United States analyzes depression across six indicators. Dr. Jean Twenge says that:

> Across all six items, depression has skyrocketed in just a few years, a
> trend that appears among blacks, whites, and Hispanics, in all regions
> of the United States, across socioeconomic classes, and in small towns,
> suburbs, and big cities.[19]

Changes like this don't just happen. If there had been a 15% increase over the same amount of time, researchers would be clamoring to find out what was causing it. When we see a 200% increase, we must acknowledge that something significant and catastrophic was injected into the culture of this generation. This has led many to develop hypotheses as to why this number began to change so suddenly and significantly.

Self-Harm

In the past mental health was a taboo topic that most individuals were reluctant to discuss. Thankfully those with mental health challenges can now talk more freely about the difficulties they are enduring. Some have hypothesized that the changes around depression and anxiety are just the result of this new openness and awareness. By examining behavioral

---

19 Jean M. Twenge, *iGen: Why Today's Super-Connected Kids Are Growing up Less Rebellious, More Tolerant, Less Happy – and Completely Unprepared for Adulthood* (New York: Atria Books, 2017), 102.

data, however, we can see that this is not the case. This data shows that people are doing more than just talking about mental health more—they are harming themselves at an ever-increasing rate.

The National Electronic Injury Surveillance System - All Injury Program (NEISS-AIP) is a dataset that collects information around first-time visits to the emergency room for a collection of representative hospitals across the United States. While it tracks many different types of injuries, I'll focus on injuries related to self-harm. In 2017 a research letter published by the Journal of the American Medical Association (JAMA) highlighted the significant change that has occurred in data between 2001 and 2015.[20]

When we examine the data included in this research letter, we see something very troubling for girls. Between 2001 and 2015 there was a 166% increase in non-fatal self-harm incidents among girls aged 10–14. But this doesn't tell the whole story. Most of this change happened between 2009 and 2015, with a 189% change happening between those years. This significant change began during the inflection point when smartphones were rapidly increasing in adoption. Something terrible is happening to preteen and early-teen girls when smartphones and social media are injected into their lives.

The data also points out something interesting for boys: whatever change caused a huge spike in self-harm for girls only minimally affects the boys. The data for boys between 2001 and 2015 remained relatively unchanged.

Suicide
While trends in self-harm are heavily weighted to one gender, the same cannot be said for suicide. Between 2000 and 2007 the suicide rate for ten-to-twenty-four-year-olds in the United States was steady, but it

---

20 Melissa C. Mercado et al., "Trends in Emergency Department Visits for Nonfatal Self-inflicted Injuries Among Youth Aged 10 to 24 Years in the United States, 2001-2015," *JAMA* 318, no. 19 (2017): 1931–1933. doi:10.1001/jama.2017.13317.

seems that something significant started to happen in 2007. In the ten years that followed, this rate jumped by 57%.[21]

While the increase in suicide has affected both genders, it does appear that preteen and teenage girls are the hardest hit by this change. Since 2007 the suicide rate for ten-to-fourteen-year-old girls has risen by an average of 12.7% per year. The boys in this age group have been affected too. They have seen a 7.1% increase every year. If we look at the next age bracket, fifteen-to-nineteen-year-olds, the changes are significant as well, with a 7.9% increase for girls and a 3.5% increase for boys. While suicide rates have always been higher for boys, the years since 2007 have greatly reduced that gap.

Age Range	Gender	Average Yearly Percentage Increase
10–14 years	Male	7.1%
	Female	12.7%
15–19 years	Male	3.5%
	Female	7.9%

Figure 2: Trends in suicide among youth ages 10 to 19 in the United States from 2007 to 2016[22]

By examining the data on both self-harm and suicide, we have statistical proof that the decline in mental health is about much more than just perception. Every indicator points toward a crisis of mental health

21 Sally C. Curtin, "State Suicide Rates Among Adolescents and Young Adults Aged 10–24: United States, 2000–2018," *National Vital Statistics Reports* 69, no. 11, 3. https://stacks.cdc.gov/view/cdc/93667.

22 Donna A. Ruch et al., "Trends in Suicide Among Youth Aged 10 to 19 Years in the United States, 1975 to 2016," *JAMA Network Open* 2, no. 5 (2019): e193886. doi:10.1001/jamanetworkopen.2019.3886.

since the time an entire generation of young people had a smartphone placed in their hands.

WHEN IS SOCIAL MEDIA OKAY?

One Sunday, when I was walking into the student ministry section of our church, I overheard two sixth graders in an intense discussion about social media. The first girl was expressing sorrow that the other one wasn't allowed on social media. The second girl was explaining the PowerPoint presentation she had developed to help convince her parents to relent and let her have an Instagram account. Together, the two girls were fine-tuning their arguments like attorneys, preparing for oral arguments before the Supreme Court.

I've had multiple parents share a similar story. Their child has begged, pleaded, and bargained for a chance to create accounts on Instagram, TikTok, and Snapchat. The social fabric of their generation is woven through these platforms, and those who are left out feel as though they have been excommunicated. These feelings are raw and real, but so are the risks they face by creating these accounts.

Teaching your child to avoid the pitfalls of social media is a part of your God-given calling to "bring them up in the discipline and instruction of the Lord" (Ephesians 6:4b). Should your child be on social media? *It depends.*

Universal Recommendations

When it comes to social media, I know that every circumstance is different. While you will have to use your best judgment as parents, I want to provide some guidelines for you, so you don't have to start from scratch. You will ultimately have to decide what rules to put in place for your own family, but it is my hope that you will seriously consider these recommendations for your home.

NO ONE SHOULD HAVE A SOCIAL MEDIA ACCOUNT BEFORE THE AGE OF THIRTEEN.

Social media use continues to trend younger. According to a recent poll, 49% of ten-to-twelve-year-olds are using social media,[23] even though all major social media platforms require new users to be at least thirteen years old. This is the case because of the Children's Online Privacy Protection Act (COPPA) law in the United States. For many of these social media platforms, simply entering a birth date or checking a box is the only verification they require.

Setting all legal issues aside, social media is too manipulative a tool to be used under the age of thirteen. Children can't yet combat the temptations it provides or counteract the insecurities it magnifies. Bullies, critics, predators, and scammers are all regular cast members on social media, and it is unfair to expect preteens to deal with the challenges they create.

Having a social media account prior to the age of thirteen also creates a moral issue. Most kids seeking social media accounts are very aware of the minimum legal age for accounts. If you have permitted your child to create an account before they hit this age, I recommend you explain to them that this wasn't the correct decision. We need to model the biblical standard of truthfulness. If this is your situation, you now have an opportunity to explain to your child that even parents can make mistakes.

If your child is over the age of twelve, it does not automatically mean that they should be leveraging social media. In a recent interview, United States Surgeon General Vivek Murthy stated that parents should band together to consider a strategy of delayed access:

23 "Sharing Too Soon? Children and Social Media Apps," *Mott Poll Report* 39, no. 4 (October 2021), http://mottpoll.org/reports/sharing-too-soon-children-and-social-media-apps.

I, personally, based on the data I've seen, believe that 13 is too early . . . If parents can band together and say you know, as a group, we're not going to allow our kids to use social media until 16 or 17 or 18 or whatever age they choose, that's a much more effective strategy in making sure your kids don't get exposed to harm early.[24]

You will have to evaluate your child's maturity and the inherent dangers of social media to determine when your child should have access. As a part of the Action Plan for this chapter, you will see the DigitalParenting.com age recommendations for joining different social media platforms.

In our home, we won't be allowing our children to be on any social media platforms before they turn sixteen. Even at that point, we plan to limit their access to specific platforms. We have been upfront with our kids on this, so this won't be a surprise to them.

IF YOUR CHILD ALREADY STRUGGLES WITH DEPRESSION, ANXIETY, OR ADDICTION, SOCIAL MEDIA SHOULD BE AVOIDED.

If your child is already dealing with complex mental health challenges, I would postpone any permission to get them onto social media. If they are already on social media, I would schedule an appointment with a mental health professional to determine if that access should continue. Given the ability of social media to amplify loneliness, depression, and anxiety, your child may be at significant risk to its dangers.

---

24 Allison Gordon and Pamela Brown, "Surgeon General Says 13 Is 'Too Early' to Join Social Media," *CNN*, January 29, 2023. https://edition.cnn.com/2023/01/29/health/surgeon-general-social-media/index.html.

SOCIAL MEDIA USE SHOULD BE LIMITED.

I described the amplifying effect of screen time on the dangers facing your child in Step 1. This is especially true when it comes to social media. In short, more time on social media means that the risks to your child are greater. One study from the UK found that fourteen-year-old girls who spent between 3 and 5 hours a day on social media had a 26% increase in depressive symptoms versus those who spent only 1 to 3 hours per day on social media. For fourteen-year-old boys there was a 21% increase of depressive symptoms when spending 3 to 5 hours a day on social media.[25] By reducing the amount of time your child spends on social media, you greatly reduce their risk of depression.

As we've already discussed, social media use falls under recreational screen time. If you have already implemented your Family Screen Time Plan, you already have a basic framework for the time your child has available to be on social media. If you are following the time recommendations that are included in Step 1, your child won't have more than one hour of social media use on any given day.

While it may be difficult to track and enforce this limit, there are tools that can help ensure that social media use stays within an acceptable range. Please see the online resources for this chapter to view up-to-date instructions on putting these into place.

IF YOUR CHILD IS ON SOCIAL MEDIA, YOU WILL NEED TO HAVE REGULAR CHECK-INS.

Just because you have followed the previous guidelines, this does not mean that your child will be exempt from the dangers of social media. The threats posed by social media still exist, even for older teens who

---

25 Yvonne Kelly et al., "Social Media Use and Adolescent Mental Health: Findings From the UK Millennium Cohort Study," *EClinicalMedicine* 6, (2018): 59–68. doi:10.1016/j. eclinm.2018.12.005.

use social media in a limited capacity. If you allow them to use social media, they will need you to instruct them on how to evaluate its effects on their mental health. This can be made possible through regularly scheduled conversations.

I have included a discussion guide in the online resources for this chapter, which can guide these conversations. This will be an item on your Action Plan. If you do not have time to facilitate these discussions, I recommend you keep your child away from social media until you do.

YOU WILL NEED TO ENCOURAGE AND PRIORITIZE FACE-TO-FACE SOCIAL INTERACTION FOR YOUR CHILD OUTSIDE OF SOCIAL MEDIA.

As a part of being countercultural, it will be beneficial for you to restore some of the social aspects of youth apart from social media. Ideally there are other families that share your view of screen time and social media that you can connect with. That is one of the benefits of exploring the content of this book with a community. You will need to resist the short-term urge to let your child build relationships that are predicated on social media platforms and instead have them invest in face-to-face social experiences that lead to higher levels of long-term life satisfaction.

ACTION PLAN
Online Resources: https://dp.run/step3

Just as I have done in the two previous steps, I want to first define a goal that will guide us as we approach the Action Plan for this step:

Goal: To protect your family from digital habits that can lead to mental health challenges.

How far are you willing to go to safeguard your child's mental health? I do not take lightly that the recommendations in this Action Plan may lead to upheaval in your home. You may need to delete a social media account you previously allowed your child to have. You may need to push back a promised date for social media access. You may even need to tell your child that social media won't be a part of their lives while they are in your home.

As you decide how you will approach social media access, keep your parenting blueprint in mind. Don't give in to short-term pressure without considering the long-term consequences. Take a few minutes to review the *wants* you defined for your family. It's helpful to have those front of mind as you get started on these tasks.

Don't forget to log your completed tasks in your Action Plan Tracker.

1. CREATE A FAMILY SOCIAL MEDIA PLAN
FOR FAMILIES WITH CHILDREN CURRENTLY USING DEVICES

I realize that the following steps may seem extreme. If the risks weren't so serious, you could take a "wait and see" approach. But since the risks, especially to girls, are very severe, we must be proactive.

The Social Media Plan will help you to be intentional about parenting your child in a social media context. If your child asks you for permission to join a social media platform, you will already have an educated answer in place. It is imperative that you remain a step ahead of the dangers they will face. You have already taken a huge step by diving into this book, and you can remain ahead of the curve by staying connected to the *Digital Parenting Community*.

The plan will guide you through recommendations on the following:

- Social media platforms that you will allow your child to use and how old they will be before opening an account

- The amount of time your child will be allowed to spend on social media per day

- The devices your child will be allowed to use to access their social media accounts

- The rules your child must follow when using social media

- The regular time when you will meet with your child to discuss their social media use

Now that you have a plan in place, you will need to implement it. If your child already has a social media account and you have decided that they shouldn't be on that particular social media platform any longer, you'll need to delete their account. Don't just deactivate the account. Go ahead and delete it. I realize that this may cause tension in your home, but we want to take away the temptation for your child to access social media from another device that you do not control. If your child will remain on social media, you'll need to get those check-ins scheduled. Avoid the temptation to put these things off into the future.

*The template for your **Social Media Plan** as well as instructions for deleting social media accounts are available in the online resources for this chapter.*

2. DISCUSS SOCIAL MEDIA AND ITS DANGERS.
FOR FAMILIES WITH CHILDREN AGES 7+

It may be tempting to wait until your child has a social media account before you discuss the attending dangers with them, but I recommend having these discussions when their friends begin to get accounts. If you can help shape their perspective on social media engagement early enough, you may avoid needing to have some difficult conversations with them when they get older.

These discussions will also introduce biblical concepts that can help them evaluate how social media is impacting them and their relationship with God.

8

STEP 4

Defending against Predators

Be sober-minded; be watchful. Your adversary the devil prowls around like a roaring lion, seeking someone to devour. (1 PETER 5:8)

SELENA RODRIGUEZ, an eleven-year-old from Enfield, Connecticut, had developed an addiction to social media, despite not being old enough to legally have accounts on her social networks of choice: Instagram and Snapchat.[1] At age eleven she wasn't a newcomer to social media. Her dependence on these platforms had already been steadily growing for

---

1 "Mother Sues Meta and Snap over Daughter's Suicide," *BBC News*, January 21, 2022. http://www.bbc.com/news/world-us-canada-60091899.

two years. Her mother, Tammy, was concerned about Selena's increasing time spent on her devices and had even taken Selena's devices away from her for a time. Tammy's growing concern led her to seek mental health treatment for her daughter.

As the effects of the COVID-19 pandemic pushed people away from the physical world, Selena pushed even further into the virtual world of social media. This began to take its toll as she struggled with severe sleep deprivation and depression. In this state of mind, Selena began to be solicited by adults on Instagram and Snapchat. These men repeatedly requested that she send sexually explicit images of herself. Eventually Selena gave in. This content, as is often the case, spread rapidly. It eventually made its way to many of her classmates. In July 2021, at the age of eleven, Selena took her own life.

In the picture that was included in Selena's obituary, I saw a young girl, full of life. Her sassy pose, her wardrobe, and the peace sign she was giving the camera didn't seem at all out of place for a girl her age. Selena was only a few months younger than my own daughter at the time. As I looked at her picture, I was reminded that she would still be here if it weren't for those adults who sought to exploit her for their own perverted sexual pleasure. If you expect the tech companies who created these platforms to protect your child, Selena's short life will serve as a reminder that those expectations are dead wrong.

I hope that by reading this chapter, you will gain the information you'll need to protect your child from a world in which these dangers of real-life predators are constantly shifting and ever-increasing. You will need to understand the reality of what your child is facing, how to discuss it with them, and how to prevent predators from even starting a conversation with them.

DANGERS

In today's digital world, predators come in all shapes and sizes, and with varying motives. The traditional case of older men seeking out younger girls for sexual exploitation is still a concern, as Selena's story reminds us. The risk online remains higher for girls, with 35% of fifteen-to-seventeen-year-old girls reporting that they have received an unwanted explicit image. The same is true of 20% of the boys in the same age range.[2] In some cases, the objective is not sexual gratification but rather financial gain. This was the case for Braden Markus, whose story I shared with you in chapter 1.

Before I get to the Action Plan, I want to take a deep dive into some of the risks predators pose. We will cover many different scenarios that young people are facing today as they interact with others on digital platforms.

Soliciting Child Pornography

While abuse takes many forms, one type of exploitation is pornographic material featuring underage subjects, generally referred to as *child pornography*. If we examine the statistics in the United States, we can see that the number of those convicted for child pornography has increased by 422% between 2005 and 2019. Of those cases, one-third were Internet strangers who never even met their victim in person.[3]

In these cases, a predator builds a relationship with an underage victim. This relationship might last for months or only minutes. At some point in the online conversation, the predator requests that the child send a nude picture or video of themselves. The youth may also receive a nude image from the predator. In Selena's case, this solicitation occurred on social media, but as I'll discuss in the next section, there are also other means of communication that predators use.

Whether on social media or in an online game experience, the

---

2   Monica Anderson, "A Majority of Teens Have Experienced Some Form of Cyberbullying," *Pew Research Center*, September 27, 2018. https://www.pewresearch.org/internet/2018/09/27/a-majority-of-teens-have-experienced-some-form-of-cyberbullying/.

3   United States Sentencing Commission. "Federal Sentencing of Child Pornography: Production Offenses." October 2021. http://www.ussc.gov/sites/default/files/pdf/research-and-publications/research-publications/2021/20211013_Production-CP.pdf.

predator is often pretending to be someone other than who they truly are. This technique of using a fake identity online is commonly known as *catfishing*. A potential victim is more likely to let their guard down if an attractive person near their age reaches out than if they were a balding fifty-year-old. Predators know how to capitalize on this mindset.

These types of conversations can happen on a variety of online platforms. The conversations often start on one platform and then jump to another. Before anyone asks your child for an image of themselves, even a fully clothed image, your child should know that the answer should always be no. Once the predator has a picture of your child, it could get distributed through porn sites or even through the *dark web*, a dangerous corner of the Internet where a majority of illegal activity occurs online.

From Online to Real Life

The NBC reality show *To Catch a Predator* aired between 2004 and 2007. It highlighted that some predators were no longer satisfied with online-only interactions. Due to the rise of location-based apps and platforms, predators could now target potential victims who lived nearby. In the show predators traveled to a location, thinking they were going to meet an underage victim, only to encounter Chris Hansen, the show's host, along with local authorities who were waiting to arrest the suspect.

When the show set up a sting operation in a town, they wouldn't just have a single predator show up. Fort Myers, Florida, and Forston, Georgia, had twenty predators show up for each operation. In Mira Loma, California, fifty-one men were arrested. While this show generated its share of controversy, it proved the fact that there are far more predators seeking to victimize youth than any of us had realized.

How prevalent is predatory behavior today? In a recent study, one in five US youth (aged eight to eighteen) reported an online sexual solicitation from someone they had never met in the real world. This solicitation could include exchanging sexual images or videos, discussing sex, or engaging in sex acts online. One in ten youth from this group reported meeting someone in real life that they had met online.[4]

People They Know

It may be tempting to think the problem with predators is limited to the strangers our child may meet online, but the news tells a different story. In many cases, communication channels including text messages, messaging apps, social media, and even online gaming platforms have been used by friends, family, and other trusted adults to have an unfiltered and unmonitored conversation with vulnerable youth. These messages often start out innocently, but they can rapidly escalate into explicit discussions.

In 2019 a trusted Florida youth pastor began to use his position of authority to build a relationship with a fifteen-year-old girl in his ministry. He eventually sent explicit messages and images through a messaging app, TextNow. He instructed the girl to deny everything if anyone asked about their relationship or the messages. Thankfully, another girl in the youth group became suspicious of some of the messages the victim was receiving, and the authorities were alerted. The youth pastor is now in jail.[5]

In 2018 a twenty-seven-year-old sixth-grade teacher from Arizona encouraged her students to message her outside of class. For one thirteen-year-old boy in the class the messages escalated quickly. Because this communication channel was open, the teacher could send explicit texts and images to the student without any oversight. The teacher went on to have sexual encounters with the student on four different

---

4   Gail Hornor et al., "Online Sexual Solicitation of Children and Adolescents in a High-Risk Population," *Journal of Pediatric Health Care* 36, no. 5 (September 2022), 449–456. doi:10.1016/j.pedhc.2022.04.010.

5   "Belleview Youth Pastor Accused of Sending Sexual Texts to 15-Year-Old Girl," WKMG ClickOrlando, February 12, 2019, http://www.clickorlando.com/news/2019/02/12/belleview-youth-pastor-accused-of-sending-sexual-texts-to-15-year-old-girl/.

occasions. Eventually the student's parents discovered the messages, thanks to a parental control app they had installed on the phone. The teacher is now serving a twenty-year jail sentence.[6]

In many ways these cases are just an extension of the type of in-person predatory behavior that existed long before the Internet. This type of victimization is most often perpetrated by trusted individuals in the child's life, including family members, teachers, coaches, and pastors. The Internet just adds a new dimension to this pattern, making it much easier for the predators to gain private access to their victims.

I wish these were isolated cases, but I read hundreds of these stories while preparing to write this chapter. For each reported case, there are many more that go unreported. In our digital world, it is a reality that you must talk to your child about what they should do if someone they trust sends them an inappropriate message, photo, or video.

Sextortion

Braden Markus's story from chapter 1 is an example of a growing trend called *sextortion*. This trend has risen to the level that the United States Federal Bureau of Investigation (FBI) has launched an educational campaign to prevent vulnerable youth from falling for the scam. According to the FBI, "This increasing threat has resulted in an alarming number of deaths by suicide."[7]

The core of the problem is that once a young person gives the predator an image or video of themselves, they must choose between meeting their demands or risking the image going public. This blackmail can continue for an extended period of time, as the predator holds

---

6   Steve Helling, "Imprisoned Ariz. Teacher Who Sexually Abused Boy, 13, Is Now Tutoring Inmates in Prison," *People*, November 1, 2021. https://people.com/crime/imprisoned-ariz-teacher-who-sexually-abused-boy-13-is-now-tutoring-inmates-in-prison/.

7   Federal Bureau of Investigation. "Sextortion." Accessed April 12, 2023. http://www.fbi.gov/how-we-can-help-you/safety-resources/scams-and-safety/common-scams-and-crimes/sextortion.

all the power once the image has been sent. The FBI states that, "the offender often releases the victim's sexually explicit material regardless of whether or not they receive payment."[8]

The best weapon against sextortion is education. If your child never sends an explicit image, this is a risk they won't have to deal with.

Human Trafficking

Human trafficking is an epidemic that, at times, can be hard to believe. We would all love to live in a world where it simply did not exist, but the data gives us evidence that it is prevalent. While the nature of human trafficking makes it difficult to determine an exact number of victims, there are data points we can examine.

In the United States, the National Human Trafficking Hotline works to identify and help victims of trafficking. Since 2007 this vital service has identified 164,839 victims of trafficking.[9] Each year thousands of those victims are minors, with 2,365 identified in 2022 alone. When we take a global perspective, we see that the problem is even bigger. The International Labour Organization (ILO) estimated that in 2016 there were 4.8 million sex-trafficking victims globally, 1 million of them minors.[10]

At this point you may be wondering how this connects to your child's online world. In its current form, the entire industry is deeply reliant on the Internet. Given what I've already covered regarding predators, it should come as no surprise that 40% of sex trafficking victims

---

8   "Sextortion."

9   "National Statistics," National Human Trafficking Hotline, Accessed August 1, 2023, https://humantraffickinghotline.org/en/statistics.

10   "Global Estimates of Modern Slavery," International Labour Organization and Walk Free, 2017. http://www.ilo.org/wcmsp5/groups/public/@dgreports/@dcomm/documents/publication/wcms_575479.pdf.

are recruited online.[11] In addition, the darkest corners of the Internet are used to solicit predators to abuse these victims.

CONNECTION POINTS

The dangers and avenues for abuse are continually changing. While in-person abuse of youth remains a significant risk, the Internet has provided a mostly unmonitored connection point that predators are exploiting. When protections are placed on one platform, the predators often move to a less-guarded means of communication. If a social media site no longer works for them, they can move to a video game platform with real-time voice and text chat.

To implement the Action Plan in this chapter, you must understand the different communication channels predators can leverage and the approaches you can take to limit their access to your child on each of these platforms.

Texting

While predators can certainly contact your child through texting, this is less likely than some of the other connection points we will discuss. Text messages pass through traditional telecommunication companies (such as AT&T and Verizon here in the United States). Unlike encrypted messaging apps, the companies handling these messages can retrieve and view their content. In many cases, text messages have been subpoenaed as evidence in legal proceedings.

While strangers may not jump into this communication channel regularly, texting is a common communication channel for people we know in real life. If a teacher, pastor, or family member has a reason to use this means of communication, it could be abused. This is why it is critical to set clear boundaries around what is appropriate and

---

11 "Traffickers Abusing Online Technology, UN Crime Prevention Agency Warns," *United Nations*, October 30, 2021, https://news.un.org/en/story/2021/10/1104392.

inappropriate to send through any online communication channel, including text messages. The moment the conversation turns to something inappropriate, your child should alert you.

It is also important to note that some phones automatically default to a different messaging platform. As an example, you can enable iMessage (a completely different technology than traditional text messaging) on iPhones and iPads. The process for configuring who can reach out to your child will vary, depending on the platform your child is using.

Phones and service providers may provide different mechanisms for limiting who can contact your child via text message. We will cover many of the most common use cases in the online material for this chapter.

Phone Calls

Traditional phone calls have become less popular, thanks to texting and other means of communication, but you should still consider setting controls on who can call your child. Just as with text messaging, these calls are tracked by the service provider, and because of that traceability, predators don't use this means of communication as often.

It is important to realize that phones can make voice calls in many different ways. You can have a voice-only call on an iPhone using FaceTime, for example. Many messaging and social media apps also have a voice-only option. Just because someone is talking with someone else on their phone, it does not mean that they are on a traditional phone call.

Phones and service providers may provide different mechanisms for limiting who can contact your child via phone call. We will cover many of the most common use cases in the online material for this chapter.

Messaging Apps

A vast majority of the predator cases I have reviewed in articles online involved some type of messaging app. These apps provide a communication channel that is a lot like texting but usually includes additional features. Apps like WhatsApp, Facebook Messenger, WeChat, Telegram, and Signal all fall into this category.

Many of these apps use encryption and privacy as a selling point. While these features have been used for good, predators can also use these capabilities for evil. Information shared through these apps may be difficult or even impossible to retrieve by outside parties. This is a big reason why predators prefer these channels over using a text message, which leaves a digital trail with the phone service provider.

I've seen many documented cases where a predator initially connected through texting and then requested that the victim continue the conversation on a messaging app. Teach your child that this should be a warning sign for them. If they ever encounter a request to switch a conversation to another communication channel, they should come to you directly.

One of the reasons your Family Device Plan in Step 2 included disabling the ability to install new apps without your permission is to prevent your child from installing a messaging app. Many of these apps treat parental controls like an afterthought. If your child suddenly wants to install a messaging app, you need to know why they want to install it and if someone asked them to install it. This conversation can prevent predators from being able to gain a foothold in your child's life.

Social Media

The line between social media apps and messaging apps is hard to define. Social media apps can present more of a danger, though, as they provide a way for a public conversation to transition to a private one. There have been cases where predators found their potential victims on social media, then pushed the individual into a private conversation. Selena's story from earlier in this chapter is an example of this pattern.

Apps like Snapchat, Instagram, Facebook (we have already mentioned Facebook Messenger as one of the messaging apps), X (formerly known as Twitter), and TikTok fall under the category of social media. All these also include private messaging capabilities, and each of them have different levels of parental controls.

How social media sites should be used should be defined in your Social Media Plan. If your child is on social media, you can review the online resources for this chapter to find instructions on how to control who can contact them on the most popular social networks.

Dating Apps

There is another category of apps we need to discuss: Dating apps, also known as hookup apps, have similarities to both messaging and social media apps. The purpose of these apps is to connect two people who previously had no connection. This generally means that the app is looking for people near the user's geographic location. Apps like Tinder and Bumble fit into this category.

Unfortunately I have spoken with many parents who have discovered their child was using these apps as a preteen or early teen. In some cases they have developed a relationship with an adult through one of these platforms. While this can happen with messaging apps and social media, dating apps provide a streamlined process for connecting with nearby strangers.

I want to be clear here: dating apps do have some protections in place to limit underage users, but the best way to prevent predators from gaining access to your child through these apps is to prevent them from being installed on your child's device.

For an updated list of dating apps, you can check out the online resources for this chapter. It will be up to you to determine when (if at all) you allow your child to use one of these apps while they are in your home. I don't ever recommend these apps. Because of the rampant deception and indecency demonstrated on these apps, I'll be encouraging my kids to never use them.

Video Calls

If we were to go back to 2013, the thought of teens being able to set up a real-time video chat from anywhere in the world seemed ludicrous. But in our current culture, most pre-teens and teens are well versed in video call and conferencing platforms, thanks to the remote learning months forced upon them by the pandemic. Solutions like FaceTime, Zoom, and Google Meet provide this capability across a wide range of devices. Many messaging and social media apps provide this capability as well.

Many of these platforms have legitimate uses. I know of Sunday school classes that have mid-week check-ins using Facetime. I know youth ministries that leveraged Zoom when the pandemic prevented them from meeting in person. I know teachers who provide tutoring groups via Google Meet after normal school hours. What is essential is that your child knows the boundaries for these platforms. They should never enter into a one-on-one conversation on any video platform with someone they do not know in real life. In addition, they should know which interactions should lead them to end the video call immediately. Don't wait to discuss this possibility until it happens; prepare them for it ahead of time, so they will know what to do.

Gaming Platforms

The documented cases of predators using gaming platforms are on the rise. As video games transitioned from a solo activity to a massive online experience, predators moved into the space as well. Platforms have matured to support real-time communication with both audio and video features. The Nintendo Switch, Sony PlayStation, and Microsoft Xbox all provide a way to customize the types of communication players can engage in.

What if the game you are playing doesn't support this type of communication? As I mentioned in chapter 2, Discord was created to solve this very issue. In many ways, it combines a real-time communication platform, social media platform, and messaging app. It started by enabling gamers to have voice and text chat while gaming, even if the game didn't have that capability. This means your child can interact with people while gaming, even if you have disabled that communication feature on the video game console. They just need Discord installed on their phone, tablet, or computer.

Discord is based on micro-communities called "servers." These servers are mostly policed by the members of the community. While the company behind Discord may occasionally step in to deal with an issue, I have found this to be the exception rather than the rule. In 2021 Discord implemented machine learning algorithms that identify material that is harmful to minors as well as activity that is generally associated with predators.[12] This increased safety focus is welcome, but it won't catch every predator.

Thankfully the major gaming platforms all have some limits that can be put in place for online interactions. You can find instructions on each major platform in the online resources for this chapter.

INCREASED RISKS

I hope that you are eager to dive into the Action Plan to prevent any of these crimes against your child from becoming a part of your family's story. Before we get there, though, I need to highlight that some of you will need to be even more proactive when it comes to protecting your child from predators. The risks here are not always equal. I want to share a handful of factors that could place your child in greater danger for becoming a victim of an online predator. According to a recent article in the Journal of Pediatric Health Care,[13] these factors include:

- Psychological and social problems

- Poor parent-child relationships

- Low self-esteem

- Low cognitive ability

- Depression

---

12 Julie Jargon, "Discord Chat App is Safer Now for Kids but Still Lacks Parental Controls," *The Wall Street Journal*, January 19, 2021, http://www.wsj.com/articles/discord-chat-app-is-safer-now-for-kids-but-still-lacks-parental-controls-11610805602.

13 Gail Hornor, "Online Sexual Solicitation of Children and Adolescents," *Journal of Pediatric Health Care* 34, no. 6 (2020): 610–618. doi:10.1016/j.pedhc.2020.05.008.

Here there is one additional factor that deserves special attention: If your child has already experienced sexual abuse, they are at a much greater risk of becoming a victim again.[14] If your child falls into this category, you may need to spend extra time reviewing your Action Plan and the discussion material with your child.

ACTION PLAN
Online Resources: https://dp.run/step4

I realize that, given all the risks across all the different communication channels, tackling this step can seem overwhelming. Before we dive into the specifics, I want to provide a goal that will guide us as we explore this Action Plan:

Goal: To prevent potential predators from contacting your child while also educating your child on how to avoid the most dangerous risks predators pose.

In this Action Plan, I will walk you through the actions you must take to reduce the risk as much as possible within your home. Don't forget the *wants* in your parenting blueprint as you work through these tasks, and don't forget to track your completed tasks in your Action Plan Tracker.

---

14 Jennie G. Noll et al., "Revictimization and Self-Harm in Females Who Experienced Childhood Sexual Abuse: Results from a Prospective Study," *Journal of Interpersonal Violence* 18, no. 12 (2003): 1452–71. doi:10.1177/0886260503258035.

1. BLOCK OTHERS FROM ACCESS TO YOUR CHILD ON DIGITAL PLATFORMS
FOR FAMILIES WITH CHILDREN CURRENTLY USING DEVICES

Our calling as parents to protect our children applies to game consoles, social media platforms, and even messaging apps. I recommend that you limit the types of people who can have unmonitored conversations with your child. There is still a risk of trusted individuals exploiting this relationship, but we will deal with that in the next section.

To accomplish this action, you must analyze any digital platform your child uses and create a prioritized list of how protections will be implemented. I recommend starting with the platforms that get the most use. If they have a phone, then you need to start there. If you have any concerns about your child's current conversations, have your child stop any interactions on those platforms until you can get basic protections put in place. This can be as simple as disabling specific apps.

A guide for completing this step of the Action Plan as well as instructions for limiting access on common digital platforms can be found in the online resources for this chapter.

2. WALK THROUGH THE DISCUSSION GUIDE ON PREDATORS WITH YOUR CHILD
FOR FAMILIES WITH CHILDREN AGES 9+

You may think that simply blocking access to online platforms will be enough to protect your child. Unfortunately it isn't. There have been many documented cases over the last few decades of predators leveraging a combination of online and in-person connections to take advantage of someone who was underage.

The best thing you can do for your child is to give them steps to follow when something inappropriate happens in an interaction—whether online or in person and whether it is with a stranger or someone they trust. Don't let them avoid discussing it because of the shame, confusion, or embarrassment they may feel. By discussing it with them ahead of time, you are equipping them to deal with situations they may encounter.

If your child interacts with people online, I recommend having this discussion. If they are nine or older, I recommend having this discussion. Use your discretion to determine which parts of the discussion you should share with your child, depending on their age. Having a plan in place can be vital—and they may need it sooner rather than later.

*The online resources for this chapter contain a discussion guide
to help you discuss this difficult topic with your child.*

9

STEP 5

Respecting Yourself; Respecting Others

A soft answer turns away wrath, but a harsh word stirs up anger. The tongue of the wise commends knowledge, but the mouths of fools pour out folly. (PROVERBS 15:1–2)

ADRIANA KUCH began her day on February 1, 2023, just like any other day. The fourteen-year-old high-school student in Bayville, New Jersey, had no idea that this day would forever change her life. Later that morning she was attacked in the hallway of her school in a planned ambush by other students.[1] I'm sure events like this have happened many times over

---

1   Michael Rothfeld and Christina Caron, "After Teen's Suicide, a New Jersey Community Grapples With Bullying," *New York Times*, February 13, 2023. http://www.nytimes.com/2023/02/13/nyregion/nj-teen-suicide-bullying-school.html.

the last few decades. We refer to incidents like these as bullying.

But a few aspects of this attack made this one different. As a part of the ambush, multiple bystanders recorded the event on their phones and then published it to both TikTok and Snapchat. As if that wasn't enough, one of the attackers continued to insult Adriana through text messages for more than twenty-four hours after the assault.

Adriana likely knew that within a day of the event, few people in her school—or even her state—would be ignorant of her humiliation. The video had spread across the country in a matter of hours. The attack was becoming her identity. After complaining to her boyfriend about facing that reality at school, she took her own life less than forty-eight hours after those videos were posted online.

The worst suffering didn't happen in full view of the bullies; it happened behind closed doors. She was dealing with the reality of thousands of people knowing of her victimization. Unlike the schoolyard of previous generations, the bullies couldn't see the full effect their abuse was having on her. Although there is no way of knowing if that would have made a difference, I would like to believe that in our shared humanity, most of us have a limit on the amount of pain we will knowingly inflict upon another person.

Adriana's story is just one example of how our digital communication channels have been weaponized against other humans. With no filter between our fingers and on-screen keyboards, it has become easier for someone to broadcast the vilest comments imaginable from the comfort of their own home for all the world to see. These behaviors are made possible by our growing cultural negligence when it comes to respecting others. This negligence has allowed a new threat to be born: cyberbullying.

THE BIBLICAL STANDARD

Before we explore this modern online behavioral phenomenon, it is essential to understand the biblical expectation for our interactions—online or otherwise. The book of Proverbs provides a master class on how our faith should shape our behavior toward others. I want to guide you through six foundational truths from Proverbs that should shape all of our communication, whether at work, at home, or in your Instagram comments.

WE ARE CALLED TO BRING PEACE AND NOT ANGER.

"A soft answer turns away wrath, but a harsh word stirs up anger."
(PROVERBS 15:1)

Righteous anger is in style, even when there is no righteousness to back it up. While this is true in the real world, it is best observed in the vitriol we see exchanged online. We aren't promised a world where we will always experience peace, but we are called to be the ones who bring peace to the table. This is a rare commodity online.

WE ARE CALLED TO SPEAK WISDOM AND NOT FOLLY.

"The tongue of the wise commends knowledge, but the mouths of fools pour out folly." (PROVERBS 15:2)

It is easy to jump online and see an endless stream of pointless conversations. It can be challenging to find online interactions that contain true wisdom instead of foolishness. God's expectations for us go beyond the tone or attitude of our digital communication. We are called to consider the value of the content we share as well.

Before hitting that *send* button, we should ask ourselves if what we are sharing is closer to wisdom or folly. As followers of Christ, the value of what we share online should distinguish us from the world. This may mean that we will need to spend additional time vetting the information we post to ensure that we only share accurate and valuable information with those who will see it.

WE ARE CALLED NOT TO TAKE PART IN GOSSIP OR DIVISION.

"A dishonest man spreads strife, and a whisperer separates close friends."
(PROVERBS 16:28)

As you will learn in this chapter, one aspect of cyberbullying is creating and sharing rumors. While this isn't always done with malicious intent, gossiping is strongly condemned in the Old and New Testaments.[2] It is common for rumors and secrets shared online to end friendships.

We are called to consider both the motivation and the end result of our communication. If somewhere deep in our heart we realize that we are trying to create strife, confrontation, or division for its own sake, we must abstain from hitting that *send* button.

This certainly isn't to say that we must avoid difficult topics. Sharing the gospel often leads to difficult conversations. We should be wise in our approach to these conversations as well as in the venue we choose for them. Many difficult conversations are more productive when held face-to-face rather than in a comment battle on Instagram, Facebook, or YouTube.

WE ARE CALLED NOT TO DELIGHT WHEN PEOPLE AROUND US STUMBLE.

"Do not rejoice when your enemy falls, and let not your heart be glad when he stumbles." (PROVERBS 24:17)

In today's digital world, we can scour social media and find numerous examples of people expressing their glee at the downfall of others. All it seems to take is someone disagreeing with our opinion,

---

2   See Prov 20:19, Rom 1:29, 2 Cor 12:20.

and we feel justified in causing their downfall. This happens at such a frenzied pace, that it is hard to track who we should be canceling today.

In God's word we see another plan for dealing with those who disagree with us. In Paul's letter to the Romans, he instructs them to "Bless those who persecute you; bless and do not curse them."[3] We can no longer treat the downfall of those who disagree with us as a spectator sport. Following the way of Christ means that we must seek to "overcome evil with good."[4]

WE ARE CALLED TO SHOW RESTRAINT.

"A fool gives full vent to his spirit, but a wise man quietly holds it back."
(PROVERBS 29:11)

We've all seen it. A social media post that is simply begging for you to reply with your best snarky response. Maybe it is someone expressing a different political view than your own, someone making fun of your beliefs, or someone downplaying your favorite athlete's achievements. Even if we choose to refrain from replying to 99% of these posts, most of us have had a moment when we wrote out a response in anger and then hit the *send* button.

The biblical requirement here doesn't just apply to how we reply to others; it also speaks to what we share online. This passage states, "a fool gives full vent to his spirit." There should be emotions we don't tweet, criticisms we don't post, and frustrations we don't express. This is what Proverbs says a wise man will do.

Should we never express ourselves online? Scripture calls us to carefully consider all that we say; this is true whether we are online or in person. We should choose our words carefully in full view of the

---

3   See Rom 12:14.

4   See Rom 12:21b.

other God-given principles listed here. If we can honestly say that our response or post exemplifies the principles listed and honors God, we can share it. This usually requires a bit of prayer and reflection, though, which requires us to move at a slower pace than the *send first, think later* approach.

WE ARE CALLED TO BE BOLD WHEN IT COMES TO THE TRUTH.

"The wicked flee when no one pursues, but the righteous are bold as a lion." (PROVERBS 28:1)

There is a reason that I chose to address this principle last. At times I have seen followers of Jesus ignore other biblical principles when they think they are being bold for the sake of the truth. Yes, God calls us to boldly stand for the truth, but He also calls us to obey the other biblical principles covered in this chapter.

In today's culture, we tend to alternate between passivity and aggression against those who question or disagree with us on topics we care about. Our goal should be to walk a path of demonstrating boldness while living in peace, speaking wisdom, unifying those around us, and not delighting in the failures of those who oppose or question us.

CYBERBULLYING

While there has been a lot of discussion around cyberbullying in our society, this term has been notoriously difficult to define. The co-founders of the Cyberbullying Research Center (CRC) define it as "willful and repeated harm inflicted through the use of computers, cell phones, and other electronic devices."[5] While these words give us a

---

5   Sameer Hinduja and Justin W. Patchin, *Bullying Beyond the Schoolyard: Preventing and Responding to Cyberbullying*, 2nd ed. (London: Corwin, 2014), 11.

working definition, we need to dive deeper to understand the common behaviors that are classified as cyberbullying.

When the Pew Research Center studied cyberbullying in 2022, they decided to focus on six key behaviors in their survey of 1,316 thirteen-to-seventeen-year-olds in the United States:[6]

- Offensive name-calling

- Spreading of false rumors about them

- Receiving explicit images they didn't ask for

- Physical threats

- Constantly being asked where they are, what they're doing, or who they're with by someone other than a parent

- Having explicit images of them shared without their consent

According to the results of this survey from the Pew Research Group, 46% of those surveyed had experienced at least one of the behaviors listed above and 28% indicated that they had been the target of multiple cyberbullying behaviors. The CRC had similar results in 2021 with 45.5% of the more than 30,000 thirteen-to-seventeen-year-olds surveyed indicating that they had been cyberbullied.[7] With nearly half of our teens affected by this, cyberbullying is a mainstream concern.

Some of these behaviors can be seen publicly. If you spend much time on social media, you will see name-calling, rumors being spread, and even physical threats being made. Other behaviors are harder to see. Sending explicit images or being continually harassed about one's

---

6   Emily A. Vogels, "Teens and Cyberbullying 2022," *Pew Research Center*, December 15, 2022, http://www.pewresearch.org/internet/2022/12/15/teens-and-cyberbullying-2022/.

7   Justin W. Patchin, "Summary of Our Cyberbullying Research (2007–2021)," *Cyberbullying Research Center*, June 22, 2022, http://www.cyberbullying.org/summary-of-our-cyberbullying-research.

current location or activities generally occurs in one-on-one or small group virtual settings. When we read tragic stories of cyberbullying, often the full context of the victimization isn't known until it is too late.

Digital Impersonation

Since the social sphere of today's youth is heavily weighted toward online interactions, digital impersonation has become a real problem. In 2012 two middle school girls were taken into custody for creating a fake profile of a classmate for the sole purpose of ruining the classmate's reputation.[8] This was the first story that enabled me to fully understand the reality of this risk. Since this event, I've heard of other students using similar practices to destroy relationships or even get a student expelled from school.

Without fully understanding the moral and legal consequences of their actions, some students may even go so far as to break the law. Digital impersonation can go beyond a simple prank and be categorized as identity theft.

Cyberstalking

For most of us, our digital identities are spread out over a collection of online platforms. These different pieces can act like breadcrumbs, enabling someone to track aspects of our real-world life. When I was growing up, there were the occasional news stories about celebrities being tracked and harassed, but with the emergence of the Internet, anyone can become a victim.

While most people consider cyberstalking a sub-category of cyberbullying, it does have some unique characteristics. Perpetrators may find personal information online and use that to threaten or manipulate others. A perpetrator may show up unannounced at an event because

---

8   Kashmir Hill, "Middle School 'Mean Girls' Face Felony Charge For Fake Facebook Account," *Forbes*, August 1, 2012. http://www.forbes.com/sites/kashmirhill/2012/08/01/mean-girls-face-felony-charge-for-fake-facebook-account/.

they tracked the person's location through their online posts. According to the CRC, these are all examples of cyberstalking.[9]

A big part of protecting your child from cyberstalking has to do with limiting what information is shared online. This is such a critical area of concern that it will be covered extensively in chapter 10, where I'll be focusing on Step 6—Maintaining Security and Privacy.

Hacktivism

Over the last decade there has been an increase in public activism in most regions of the world. Much of this activism has followed the traditional methods of protests and demonstrations, however a growing number of activists have leveraged the Internet to not only express their ideas but also to harm those who disagree with them.

While online retribution can come in many different forms, *doxing* seems to be one of the most common tactics. In this approach a person's private information is leaked online. This could be a cell phone number, a home address, a social security number, or a place of work. This information is then used to threaten or harass the target virtually or even in person. This harassment can last for a day or for years. Given the availability of information on the Internet, it is much easier for hacktivists to get their hands on the private info of their targets than it has ever been before.

Hacktivism isn't limited to high-profile political or business figures. These tactics have also been employed on journalists, athletes, and even gamers who offended their virtual adversaries. It has led to protests at the person's home, continuous harassment on digital communication channels, and even false information being presented to police for the purpose of tricking law enforcement into raiding the target's house—a tactic known as *swatting*.

---

9   Sameer Hinduja, "Cyberstalking," *Cyberbullying Research Center,* Accessed March 21, 2023. http://www.cyberbullying.org/cyberstalking.

What Cyberbullying Isn't

I have spoken with parents who have used the term cyberbullying to refer to any online interaction that hurt their child's feelings. We must be very careful not to adopt this overly broad definition. Your child needs to learn to deal with hurtful words, as there will be plenty of them to deal with throughout their life. So, how do we clearly distinguish between the jerks and the cyberbullies?

One of the reasons I prefer to use the definition from the CRC[10] is that it gives us a framework to use to evaluate online interactions. It states that cyberbullying is willful. Given the lack of body language and facial expressions online, it can be easy to misinterpret someone's message. If it isn't willful, it isn't cyberbullying. The definition also states that it needs to be a repeated behavior pattern. Next, the victim must realize that they have been harmed by the interaction. Finally, it needs to happen on a digital device.

While the definition clearly states that it needs to be a repeated pattern, there are some situations where a single offense may warrant involvement from parents, school administrators, or even law enforcement. If a bully threatens physical harm, sends an explicit image, or is caught attempting to impersonate your child, I recommend taking immediate action. The information you need to effectively respond to these incidents can be found in the Action Plan for this chapter.

WHAT CHANGED?

After many conversations with parents, I've realized that the word "cyberbullying" can be a source of confusion. Often people who grew up without pervasive digital technology simply see it as today's version of bullying. I've even had a parent stand up during the question-and-answer portion of one of our live events and emphatically state, "We

---

10 Cyberbullying Research Center. "What is Cyberbullying?" Accessed March 21, 2023. http://www.cyberbullying.org/what-is-cyberbullying.

had bullying when I was a kid too, and we turned out fine. We need to stop making such a big deal about cyberbullying."

Let's take a step back and analyze the dangerous characteristics that amplify cyberbullying's potential to cause harm.

EVERYONE IS ALWAYS CONNECTED.

As I write this, I'm only a few months past my forty-second birthday. In the late '90s my high school social sphere paused at about 3 p.m. each weekday, when most of us vacated Cleveland High School and left for home. When I got home, I had another group of friends I hung out with regularly who lived within walking distance of my home. There were some overlaps in those friend groups, but if I ever needed to escape any social drama within one group, there was always another group I could connect with instead.

In today's technology-driven social world, everyone is always connected. If you experience any social drama, chances are that all your friends will know about it within minutes. While this has made the world smaller, it also has made it harder to escape the inevitable social mishaps that come with life as a teenager (or even as an adult) in today's hyper-connected world.

TECHNOLOGY NEVER SLEEPS.

In my parents' generation, if you wanted to be informed about national and global events, you watched the evening news. Broadcasters like Peter Jennings, Dan Rather, and Tom Brokaw were the gateway to the crucial news events that had happened over the last 24 hours. The year before I was born, Ted Turner launched the world's first 24-hour news network, CNN. While it took some time for a never-ending stream of news to be fully embraced by the masses, the thought that anyone would wait ten to twenty hours for critical bits of news to come out seems laughable today.

A teen's life also exists within a continual news cycle, but instead of being broadcast on CNN, Fox News, or the BBC, it is broadcast through platforms like Snapchat, TikTok, and Instagram. Their peers can speak about them at any point in a 24-hour period on a variety of mediums. In my day, the bullies rarely followed their victims home. In today's social news cycle, even normal sleeping hours can't prevent someone from being victimized.

PEOPLE CAN TALK ABOUT YOU, EVEN IF YOU AREN'T ONLINE.

When we discussed the mental health effects associated with using social media, I also alluded to the fact that you didn't have to be on a social network to be affected by it. While you can prevent your child from using social media excessively, there is no way to keep your child from being the subject of online posts, comments, or photos.

YOU CAN DESTROY SOMEONE'S LIFE, INCLUDING YOUR OWN, FROM THE COMFORT OF YOUR BEDROOM.

In-person bullying generally requires that you physically engage with the victim. As you hurl insults, you see the look on the victim's face as they process their emotions. You may see the tears welling up in their eyes, the fear as they ponder their response, or the shame that comes from being a victim. While some of these attacks can be vicious, the bully still must face the fact that they are tearing down a human being.

The *send* button is an easier adversary. In our digital world, you can think of the meanest possible thing to say to someone and send it for the whole world to see without even a second thought. Psychologists refer to this as the *online disinhibition effect*.[11] It's never been easier to tear someone down. It's also never been easier to make a poor decision that can impact the rest of your life by sharing something that is hurtful . . . and it all seems unreal because it is happening virtually.

ANONYMITY SKIRTS RESPONSIBILITY.

Interacting online offers users the ability to gain something that is hard to achieve in real life: anonymity. This can take many forms, including engaging on anonymous platforms or pretending to be someone other than yourself. The allure is to say whatever is on your mind without ever being bothered by accountability.

There is a reason why almost every anonymous social platform that has been launched on the Internet has been shut down. The freedom to post without any accountability almost always devolves into the worst human behavior can offer. Platforms like Ask.fm, After School, Secret, Yolo, and LMK all ended up shutting their virtual doors, due to external pressure.

---

11 John Suler, "The Online Disinhibition Effect," *Cyberpsychology & Behavior* 7, no. 3 (2004): 321–26. doi:10.1089/1094931041291295.

DANGERS

There was a time when the dangers of cyberbullying were not widely known. Thankfully, a lot more is known today, thanks to a whole host of studies that have analyzed its effects. Cyberbullying has now become a big enough concern in the medical community that a 2022 journal article stated that, "Primary-care physicians should screen adolescents and young adults for inappropriate or misuse of social media and cyberbullying."[12] I've already heard from multiple parents that these conversations are happening in their visits with their pre-teen's pediatrician.

Why is this such a big concern? What do these risks look like for your child? How bad can it get? As a parent, it is important to understand the answers to these questions, as they have the power to help you understand the urgency with which you should address cyberbullying in your home. Multiple studies have shown that it has effects on the victims, the perpetrators, and even the observers.

One of the challenges that comes with cyberbullying is that it is underreported. According to Dr. Pamela M. Anderson, the reasons for this are multi-faceted:

> They [the victims] feel embarrassed or ashamed to be a target. They don't want to be seen as a snitch and lose even more social status. They fear retaliation. They feel like it's their responsibility to deal with it. They don't recognize it as bullying or as something serious. In short, like adults, they don't see it as that big of a deal . . . But another very important reason is that they do not want to lose access to their technology—this lifeline to their social world.[13]

---

12 Jennifer Caceres and Allison Holley, "Perils and Pitfalls of Social Media Use: Cyber Bullying in Teens/Young Adults," *Primary Care: Clinics in Office Practice* 50, no. 1 (March 2023): 37–45. doi:10.1016/j.pop.2022.10.008.

13 Pamela M. Anderson, "Why Teens Don't Report Cyberbullying," *Youth Tech Health*, August 2, 2017, http://www.yth.org/teens-dont-report-cyberbullying/.

In many cases your reaction and response to other technology challenges can have a direct impact on whether your child sees you as a part of the solution to cyberbullying or not. How you react to cyberbullying is a big enough concern that it will be a part of the Action Plan for this chapter.

Suicide

I discussed the increasing suicide rate among youth in Step 3. Cyberbullying is merely one factor among many that are causing this alarming trend. In a 2022 study, participants who had experienced cyberbullying were four times as likely to report thoughts of suicide.[14] The same study also showed a contrast between in-person bullying and cyberbullying: unlike their in-person counterparts, the digital bullies were not at an increased risk for suicidal thoughts or attempts.

In many cases cyberbullying is made worse—either by the student not reporting the incident or by intervening adults not providing the necessary support. With only 23% of cyberbullied students reporting the incident to an adult at their school,[15] the remainder are left to deal with this trauma on their own. It is critical to prepare your child before any incident of cyberbullying takes place so that if/when it happens, they know what actions they should take. By doing so, you may help save your child's life.

Self-Harm

In addition to suicide, there is a strong correlation between cyberbullying and self-harm. In a 2021 study, it was found that the adolescents surveyed were seven times more likely to engage in non-suicidal

---

14 Shay Arnon et al., "Association of Cyberbullying Experiences and Perpetration with Suicidality in Early Adolescence," *JAMA Network Open* 5, no. 6 (June 2022): e2218746. doi:10.1001/jamanetworkopen.2022.18746.

15 Caceres and Holley, "Perils and Pitfalls of Social Media Use."

self-injury (NSSI) if they had reported any type of cyberbullying.[16] This behavior includes cutting, skin carving, burning, scratching, and biting.

Although this study had a small sample size, the results show that this behavior is common among adolescents when faced with the emotional distress of cyberbullying. If parents discover these self-injurious behaviors, they should consider them warning signs for suicide.[17]

Becoming the Bully

In traditional bullying scenarios, there is a power imbalance between the victim and the bully. You can think of the archetypal example of the larger, older student threatening the younger, smaller student into handing over their lunch money. In scenarios like these, there is a very low risk of the victim becoming a bully. The power imbalance is simply too great.

When we move to the Internet, however, the balance of power can change more quickly. If the younger, smaller student has been insulted by the larger, older student, the victim can use their understanding of social media to create a false account for the express purpose of victimizing their bully. Cyberbullying has a very low barrier of entry, and the transition from victim to bully is far easier on the Internet than it is in person.[18]

If your child is not taught how to properly deal with occurrences of cyberbullying, the approach of online vigilante justice may seem appealing to them. This is one of the many reasons why a biblical foundation is absolutely critical. In the moment of temptation, your child must remember that they are called to live by different standards: those

---

16 Elizabeth C. Lanzillo et al., "The Influence of Cyberbullying on Nonsuicidal Self-Injury and Suicidal Thoughts and Behavior in a Psychiatric Adolescent Sample," *Archives of Suicide Research* 27, no. 1 (September 2021): 156–163. doi:10.1080/13811118.2021.1973630.

17 Paul O. Wilkinson, "Nonsuicidal Self-Injury: A Clear Marker for Suicide Risk," *Journal of the American Academy of Child and Adolescent Psychiatry* 50, no. 8 (2011): 741–743. doi:10.1037/a0030278.

18 Elias Aboujaoude et al., "Cyberbullying: Review of an Old Problem Gone Viral," *Journal of Adolescent Health* 57, no. 1 (July 2015): 10–18. doi:10.1016/j.jadohealth.2015.04.011.

defined by God's word. This calling compels them to respect others, even if they have been mistreated.

Legal Issues

Countries around the world are implementing laws which focus specifically on cyberbullying. While this provides greater direction and tools for families, schools, and law enforcement, it also means that the penalties for cyberbullying have increased in certain jurisdictions far beyond what they were a decade ago. Depending on the type and frequency of online harassment, teens have been charged with everything from a misdemeanor to manslaughter.

The entire category of hacktivism creates another set of legal issues. Laws vary from state to state and from country to country, and there are many places where engaging in this behavior could get you charged with a crime. In 2018 an intern in the United States House of Representatives leaked the personal information of two congressmen during a contentious Supreme Court Justice nomination process. This intern was charged with releasing restricted personal information,[19] which is just a fancy description for doxing. The intern is now serving a four-year sentence.

RESPECT GUIDELINES

Before we get to the Action Plan, I want to review the DigitalParenting.com Respect Guidelines, which provide basic principles for governing online behavior. If you examine your parenting blueprint, you will likely find that following these guidelines will help support many of the *wants* you have defined for your family. The Action Plan will give you resources to introduce and discuss these with your child:

---

19 Emily Sullivan, "House Intern Arrested, Charged With Doxing Senator During Kavanaugh Hearing," National Public Radio, October 4, 2018, http://www.npr.org/2018/10/04/654264122/house-intern-arrested-for-reportedly-doxing-senator-during-kavanaugh-hearing.

Respect Yourself

- Understand how you should be treated online.

- Block and report people who don't show you respect online.

- Know who can see what you post.

- Don't post anything you wouldn't want all your friends or your parents to see.

Respect Others

- Pause and consider each post or message before you hit send/post/publish.

- Don't forward messages or media about other people.

- Report to your parent, guardian, or teacher if you see peers being bullied online.

- Don't share other people's pictures or posts without their express permission.

- Never take photos or videos in private places like bathrooms or changing rooms.

- Never pretend to be someone else online or use someone else's account.

- Never post on an anonymous site or social network.

ACTION PLAN
Online Resources: https://dp.run/step5

As parents, you can make a substantial difference in this area of your child's life by your example of self-control and by intentional education. Studies have shown that cyberbullying educational efforts are effective at reducing incidents in a school setting. They will be even more effective within a household where the respect guidelines are modeled regularly. Before we dive into the specifics, let's analyze the goal for this Action Plan:

> **Goal**: To lead your child to respect others in their online interactions while also giving them a plan for what to do if they or someone they know is being cyberbullied.

To make this goal a reality, you will have to educate yourself, teach your child what the Bible says, and have an open discussion on respect. Let's walk through each of these in turn. Don't forget to update your Action Plan Tracker as you complete these tasks.

1. REVIEW OUR PARENT'S GUIDE TO CYBERBULLYING
FOR ALL FAMILIES

When it comes to cyberbullying, the first step for parents is education. You need to understand what to look for, what to do, and how to prevent it from affecting your child. As a part of our online resources for this chapter, I have consolidated many different resources to help equip you into our *Parent's Guide to Cyberbullying*. This resource will require some homework on your part. You will need to dive into the specifics of your region's laws as well as your child's school policies on bullying.

While we want to prevent cyberbullying wherever possible, your child may still be affected. Having the necessary information about local laws and school policies about cyberbullying is essential for parents. With this information in hand, you can make a more informed decision if your child is ever a victim or perpetrator of cyberbullying. This guide will also help you understand how you can increase the likelihood of your child coming to you if they are ever affected by cyberbullying in any way.

*You can find our **Parent's Guide to Cyberbullying***
in the online resources for this chapter.

2. REVIEW THE BIBLE STUDY ON RESPECTING OTHERS
FOR FAMILIES WITH CHILDREN AGES 9+

The included Bible study will help you lead your child through the biblical expectations for communication from the book of Proverbs covered earlier in this chapter. As you are walking your child through this study, take time to analyze your own online behavior and note areas of improvement. This biblical foundation will help prepare your child for the guidelines we will be covering in the next action.

The Bible study guide on respect is available in
the online resources for this chapter.

3. REVIEW THE RESPECT DISCUSSION GUIDE WITH YOUR CHILD.
FOR FAMILIES WITH CHILDREN AGES 9+

The *Respect Discussion Guide* walks you through eleven guidelines your child can use to respect themselves and others. The guide also provides scenarios to help you discuss how these points can be applied to online interactions in practical ways. You may need to tailor the discussion to the age of your child, but the end goal is the same. You want your child to know how to respond before they are put into the situation.

> The **Respect Discussion Guide** *is included in the online resources for this chapter.*

10

STEP 6

Maintaining Security and Privacy

Behold, I am sending you out as sheep in the midst of wolves, so be wise as serpents and innocent as doves. (MATTHEW 10:16)

IT'S A FEW MINUTES BEFORE 9 A.M., and a text message from an unknown number pops up on my phone. It's telling me that I need to act urgently, because my Netflix account is now on hold, due to a problem with my billing information. The message includes a handy link I can click to resolve this payment issue. There's only one problem: I don't have a Netflix account. This message is one of many scam messages that make its way into the Messages app on my phone every day.

147

Next, I check the headlines for the day. I see that the debate over TikTok has reached a fever pitch here in the United States. Congress spent hours questioning the organization's current CEO, Shou Zi Chew, over multiple data privacy concerns. In addition, there were concerns over whether the government of China could improperly use the data collected from the platform.

Later the same morning I visit the website of a cruise line that operates here in the United States. My family and I had an amazing time on a cruise earlier in the year, so I decided to review some other destinations. After reviewing the options, I close the website to dive into work. Moments later, I notice that someone is trying to reach me on my phone. As I look at the caller ID, I see that the cruise line is calling me. Their marketing technology is smart enough to know that I was the one exploring new cruise ideas, even though I hadn't logged in to their website.

While the Internet is no longer limited to those with high levels of technical expertise, the level of wisdom and discernment required to operate safely online has never been higher. Those technically proficient members of your family have likely graduated from just helping with printer problems to helping loved ones evaluate text messages and emails to determine their validity.

Do you know what else has never been higher? The amount of data that is collected about our online behaviors. While TikTok is concerning, due to the sheer amount of user data that is collected, they are not alone. A great deal of information about our behaviors and preferences is constantly being collected, so that organizations can target us with advertisements. After all, the best time to tell someone about a discount on new cruises is right after they spent time salivating over new cruise destinations on the company's website.

If technology will be a part of your child's life, I highly recommend that you teach them how to operate safely online. While your child should obviously steer clear of the many opportunities for sin online, they should also be aware that people will be trying to steal their money, attention, and private data.

BIBLICAL PRIVACY

Before we examine the dangers we face and the practices that can protect us, it is critical that we understand what the Bible says about privacy. In this digital world, many have used online privacy as a means of covering up their actions. They want to be able to look at porn, engage in sinful experiences, and even engage in illegal activity without suffering any real-world consequences, but as Christians we know that this is a futile effort. God sees all and knows all.

The Gospel of Luke states:

> Nothing is covered up that will not be revealed, or hidden that will not be known. Therefore whatever you have said in the dark shall be heard in the light, and what you have whispered in private rooms shall be proclaimed on the housetops. (Luke 12:2–3)

When I refer to privacy in this book, I am referring to the desire to control at some level what companies, governments, and even strangers know about our personal lives. In no way does this negate our calling to live in Christian community, pursue righteousness, and be accountable for our actions. Just as it is true of most of the topics covered in this book, followers of Jesus are called to be countercultural in this area.

DANGERS

Before we examine the practices that will enable your child to operate safely and securely online, I want to review a few of the digital dangers that exist. By more fully understanding these dangers, you will have a better grasp of the urgency to properly equip both yourself and your child for the online world in its current form.

Identity Theft

The Internet's increasing popularity has brought with it an increase in identity theft. No longer do perpetrators have to steal mail from your mailbox to apply for a credit card in your name. The Internet provides a vast treasure trove of personal information that has made this a more commonplace occurrence. You may think that this is primarily a problem for adults, but that isn't the case.

Identity fraud affects one out of fifty children in the United States, costing nearly $1 billion annually.[1] One of the reasons this is such a problem is that it can often go undetected until the child goes to apply for financial aid for college, a car loan, or to get an apartment lease. Identity theft often causes significant damage to the child's credit.

There are many ways that identity theft can occur: some are things you can control, and others are simply an inevitable result of our digital world. Stop and think for a moment about everyone who has your personal information. In the United States this may mean your social security number, date of birth, and phone number. It's scary what someone can do if they have all of this information.

Data breaches can expose this information anywhere it is stored: this includes schools, doctor's offices, and even credit agencies. In most cases, you cannot control the data these types of organizations store, but there are plenty of other areas where we can exercise caution and prudence when it comes to sharing our personal information.

Financial Loss

Losing the battle to maintain privacy and security can cost you. How much? In 2021 consumers in the United States lost $5.8 billion to fraud, much of which was facilitated through online communication channels. According to the US Federal Trade Commission:

> Imposter scams were the most prevalent form of fraud in 2021 . . . the typical victim lost $1,000. In such scams, criminals pretend to be someone else to steal money or sensitive personal information. They

---

1 Tracy Kitten, "Child Identity Fraud: A Web of Deception and Loss," *Javelin*, November 2, 2021. http://www.javelinstrategy.com/research/child-identity-fraud-web-deception-and-loss.

may include romance scams, as well as people falsely claiming to be a government official, a relative in distress, a well-known business or a technical support expert . . .[2]

Learning to distinguish between authentic and fake communications may be one of the best investments of your time. By understanding the flags to watch for, you can keep your personal resources away from the thieves who are trying to steal them from you.

Data Loss

In college we used external hard drives to store our project work. This was long before the cloud-based storage many leverage today. We carried these drives to the computer lab every time we worked on our assignments. One day during my senior year, a classmate accidentally tripped over the cable connecting his hard drive to the computer. His firewire hard drive flew off the desk and hit the floor hard while the cable violently ejected from the computer. With a growing sense of dread, he fearfully plugged the cable back into the computer, only to discover that all his data was gone. There wasn't a backup. His nearly completed senior project was gone forever.

You may be able to identify with his pain. In a 2022 survey, 54% of the respondents reported having lost some of their personal data. But despite this risk, only 10% of those surveyed are backing up their data daily.[3]

What data do you never want to lose? Is it those engagement pictures, the videos of your child's first steps, or that voicemail of a loved one who has since passed away? The more we live our lives through

---

2   Greg Iacurci, "Consumers Lost $5.8 Billion to Fraud Last Year — up 70% over 2020," *CNBC*, February 22, 2022. http://www.cnbc.com/2022/02/22/consumers-lost-5point8-billion-to-fraud-last-year-up-70percent-over-2020.html.

3   Yev Pusin, "The 2022 Backup Survey: 54% Report Data Loss with Only 10% Backing Up Daily," *Backblaze*, June 16, 2022. http://www.backblaze.com/blog/the-2022-backup-survey-54-report-data-loss-with-only-10-backing-up-daily/.

digital devices, the more our treasured possessions will span the digital and physical worlds. Everyone should have a plan for backing up what is most important to them.

The urgency of this is compounded by emerging trends like *ransomware*. Ransomware, a type of digital extortion, takes over a computer and forces the victim to pay money to have their computer unlocked in order to regain access to their personal data. While ransomware generally affects businesses, individuals have also fallen prey to it. If you don't have your data backed up, you may permanently lose access to it through ransomware, even if you choose to pay the digital ransom to the terrorists controlling your devices.

PRIVACY AND SECURITY PRACTICES

Dealing with the evolving threats on the Internet can seem like playing a game of whack-a-mole. Each time we figure out how to smash one threat, another two pop up to take its place. While the threats can continually change, a basic set of online safety practices can guide what you and your child do online and ensure that you stay protected from many of the digital dangers I have covered in this chapter.

These seven practices are designed for both you and your child. They are meant to be paired with the online resources for this chapter. As you read about these practices, you will likely ask yourself, "How do I do that?" That's to be expected. That is why each principle will have its own corresponding how-to guide in the online resources for this chapter. They will answer that very question.

Don't Overshare

It doesn't take long to find someone who shares way too much information online. Some feel that it is their responsibility to share every meal, relationship struggle, political viewpoint, and work frustration with the world. While it may seem annoying, it can actually be dangerous. Predators and scammers can piece together far more than you might think from your online posts.

KEEP PRIVATE INFORMATION PRIVATE.

One of the best things you can do for your child is to teach them what should remain private. Even though they may not be doing anything wrong by sharing information, their choice can have far-reaching consequences. While there may be reasons for adults to share sensitive information online (while shopping online, filing their taxes, or signing up as a new patient for a medical provider, for example), your child needs to know that they should never share sensitive information online. Giving your home address to Amazon.com and giving it to a stranger on Discord are two very different things.

Here are some examples of information your child should know to never share online:

- Phone number

- Identification numbers (such as your social security number in the United States)

- Home address

- School information

- Birth date

- Current location

We also need to teach them that they can accidentally leak this information if they don't fully think through their posts. Even if your child follows this rule, I suggest you employ these additional safety measures as a precaution.

DISABLE LOCATION DATA FOR MOST APPLICATIONS.

Take a minute and think about which applications on your phone really need your location information. While it makes sense for Google

Maps to have that information, for example, it doesn't make sense for social media apps to have it. When it comes to your child, you need to be proactive about ensuring that only a small handful of applications have access to this personal information.

Limit Your Audience

You can learn a lot about the world by simply sitting back and watching interactions on Facebook. As more and more of the fifty-and-older crowd began to pour into Facebook, it became painfully obvious that many of them didn't fully realize the reach of each of their posts. Some grandparents posted on their grandchild's timeline, thinking it was a private message. Sometimes they posted information that these family members didn't want the entire world to see. Many of them used the default privacy settings, which made this information available to more users than they ever realized.

ENSURE PRIVACY SETTINGS ARE PROPERLY CONFIGURED FOR ALL ONLINE COMMUNITIES.

Unfortunately, few social media users of any age are aware of who can see their posts. While they may have tweaked the privacy settings when they first created their account, they haven't revisited them in years. *Do you know who can see your posts?*

While adults may have valid reasons for opening their posts to the world, minors should always avoid this. Everyone can benefit from reviewing the privacy settings every year for each of their social media accounts, so they can know the reach of their posts.

Keep Accounts Secure

Ian wants to simplify his life. He decides to hire a locksmith to change his home, car, office, gym locker, and even his parents' home locks to all use the same universal key. He also decides to get fifty copies of this key made, so that he can have ready access to another key if he loses one. After a few weeks, Ian realizes that he has already lost four keys. Does Ian have a problem?

Ian isn't real, but Ian's story demonstrates a reality many people create: some very sensitive online information is safeguarded by a single password that has been used over and over. As more companies experience data breaches, it has been revealed that some of them store passwords in such a way that hackers can steal them. Hackers regularly take these stolen credentials and attempt to log in to common sites like banks, social media platforms, and streaming media apps.

USE UNIQUE PASSWORDS STORED IN A PASSWORD MANAGER.

Imagine that Ian hadn't configured each lock to use the same key. Imagine that instead each lock required a different key. Would the risk be greater or smaller if he then lost a key? Obviously, the risk decreases if each key works with just a single lock. In today's digital world we should follow the same concept: each online account should use a unique password.

How can anyone keep track of all of these passwords? Password managers exist to solve this problem. Thankfully, there are many different options to choose from, including some solid free options. These password managers handle the entire process for you—from creating a random password to filling in that password when you come back to log in to the site. I even use one that lets me share passwords with my wife, so she can easily access our shared accounts.

At this point you may be asking how you can know that password managers are safe to use. After all, if someone steals the data in your password manager, don't they still have access to all of your data? Most password managers are encrypted in such a way that there has to be a master password to unlock your password data. If a hacker steals your password data, they still cannot get into your saved passwords without this virtual key. That being said, not all password managers are equally as safe, so be sure to review the recommended password managers in the online resources for this chapter.

As you go about implementing this principle in your home, it is important to categorize your online accounts. Think of any account that has access to your most sensitive information. This includes banking information and government identification numbers. These should be the sites you integrate into your password manager first. After this, you can add in sites that have your health and payment information. Once that is complete, you can add in additional sites as you use them.

When it comes to password safety, it is important to remember that longer is always better. Having a longer password that is easier for you to remember is better than having a shorter password with a bunch of random symbols. If you are using a password manager, have it generate long passwords for each of the accounts you are managing. I usually default to twenty characters unless the site requires shorter ones.

USE MULTI-FACTOR AUTHENTICATION.

Next, let's imagine that Ian had to use both a key and his fingerprint to get into his home. Would this make it easier or harder for thieves to get into the house? Clearly this would make it more difficult for others to gain access. It also adds another step that Ian will have to follow, but there is no doubt that his home is now more secure.

When we add an additional step to our online accounts beyond just a username and a password, this is referred to as multi-factor authentication (MFA). You may also see it called two-factor authentication (2FA). These additional factors can be a code sent to your phone as a text message or a generated code from an authenticator app on your device. This additional step provides another level of security that is much harder to hack. Adding MFA is essential for the accounts holding your most sensitive information. Many password managers include tools that make it even easier to adopt MFA on popular platforms. While you will still have to configure MFA on the site or app, the password manager can do the heavy lifting of generating codes for you.

DON'T SHARE LOGIN INFORMATION.

Ever since the rise in popularity of streaming services like Netflix and Hulu, password sharing has become popular again. While there are serious ethical concerns around this behavior, the risk is relatively low. If a friend is sharing your account, they might have the ability to upgrade or cancel the billing plan. Unfortunately I've also seen people use password sharing for their work and financial accounts. The risks here are exponentially higher. I recommend never sharing login information for these types of accounts with anyone but your spouse.

At times your child may be tempted to share their login information with friends. They need to know that this information should be considered just as sensitive as their home address or their social security number. They should not share this information with anyone but you. In addition, they shouldn't try to log in to their accounts on their friends' devices. Some platforms save the login credentials, and this could enable the friend to later access the platform under your child's account. In many digital impersonation cases, account access was gained in this way. What seemed harmless at the time ended up causing tremendous harm.

DON'T USE EASILY GUESSABLE SECURITY QUESTIONS.

Some sites offer security questions as a way of restoring your access if you forget your password. It is important to treat the answers to these questions like they are a type of password. If you have a list of possible security questions, try to pick the questions that are the hardest for others to guess. Most of your Facebook friends may know the name of your elementary school, but they won't likely know the town where your mother was born. Strive to use questions that only you can answer.

Secure Your Devices
I've had a chance to drive through the American West, and there are some towns in Wyoming and Idaho where I suspect people don't even

bother to lock their doors. These charming towns with a few hundred people have homes spaced so far apart that you have to hike to even get to your neighbor's house.

Some friends of mine purchased a home in downtown Chattanooga right at the beginning of the city's revitalization. While people think of the Tennessee Aquarium, Lookout Mountain, and Ironman races when they think of downtown Chattanooga, there was a time when crime and pollution were the hallmarks of this city. When I first visited my friends' home, I was reminded of this by the heavy iron bars on the windows and the heavy front door they kept locked at all hours of the day.

When it comes to operating online, we must remember that we are all on the rough side of town. To protect our devices, data, and sanity, we will need to use our own heavy iron bars to keep unwanted intruders out.

ALWAYS LIMIT ACCESS TO YOUR DEVICES.

Every device you own must have a password, passcode, or biometric (facial detection, fingerprint) login. No one should be able to easily access the data on your devices. I've known adults who have purposefully removed any barriers on their devices because they wanted to be able to easily hand them off to their child or grandchild. This is a mistake.

USE ANTI-MALWARE PROTECTION.

Computer viruses are created to cause havoc on our devices, but viruses are only one type of *malware*. Wikipedia defines malware as:

> Any software intentionally designed to cause disruption to a computer . . .
> Researchers tend to classify malware into one or more sub-types
> (i.e. computer viruses, worms, Trojan horses, ransomware, spyware,

adware, rogue software, wiper and keyloggers).[4]

While I could write a whole chapter on each type of malware, I want to address these risks together. The best defense against malware includes following good general security practices as well as using anti-malware software.

Different platforms (Mac, Windows, iOS, Android) have different tools when it comes to anti-malware software. I invite you to review the online resources for this chapter to determine what you'll need to put in place on your specific devices.

NEVER GIVE A FRIEND ACCESS TO YOUR DEVICES.

Just as we discussed not giving a friend access to our accounts, the same should be true for our devices. No one should be able to have access to your child's device except for you. While it might be tempting for your child to give a best friend access to their phone, this can create security vulnerabilities. Am I saying that your child can't let a friend call their parents on your child's phone? Not at all. I'm saying that the friend shouldn't have the passcode to your child's phone.

ONLY INSTALL APPLICATIONS
FROM TRUSTED SOURCES.

Applications that are installed on your computer, tablet, or phone have special access to your data. In most cases, that isn't a problem. If you install Photoshop from Adobe's website or Chrome from Google's site, you can have a high level of confidence that the application is legitimate. If you download an application from a random website, however, you don't have those assurances. It is essential that you download any

___

4   Wikipedia. "Malware." Last updated March 12, 2023. https://en.wikipedia.org/wiki/Malware.

of your applications directly from the company that created them.

Don't be tempted to install Microsoft Office from a random site that isn't controlled by Microsoft itself. While Microsoft, Google, Amazon, and Apple are implementing more controls and safeguards to make sure malware disguised as a regular application doesn't end up causing issues on your machine, you still need to be diligent about every app you install.

When you download and use a hacked version of paid software, it is called *pirating*. While pirating is always unethical and illegal, it is also dangerous. Many pirated movies, songs, and applications have been infected with malware. As is so often the case, the honest, biblical approach is also the safest: Completely avoid pirated media and applications.

ENCRYPT YOUR DEVICE.

In elementary school I remember two girls in my class who passed notes to each other during class. To prevent anyone else from reading these notes, they used a secret code to communicate with each other. This is very similar to the concept of encryption. If someone takes your actual phone, laptop, or tablet, can they get to your data? If your device is unencrypted, the answer is *yes*.

Thankfully most devices are encrypted by default. If you are installing a new operating system on a home computer, it may ask you if you want to encrypt the disk. Your answer to this question should always by *yes*. For instructions on how to determine if your current devices are already encrypted as well as how to encrypt them if they are not, please review the online resources for this chapter.

Protect Your Finances

I'm old enough to remember when people thought e-commerce was an outlandish concept. I recall more than one person asking who would ever be dumb enough to put their credit card information into a website.

If we fast-forward to today, many of the physical stores that were a mainstay of our pre-Amazon lives no longer exist.

Most of those former e-commerce naysayers are likely Amazon Prime members today, but they weren't entirely wrong about having concerns. Every time we submit our financial information to the Internet, there is a risk. So how do we protect our money in our digital world?

AVOID UNKNOWN ONLINE VENDORS.

During one of my visits to my in-laws, I was asked about a site that was offering power tools at unbelievably low prices. I don't know if you've priced out any Milwaukee power tools recently, but let's just say quality power tools are far from cheap. This site had several red flags. There were a few instances of broken English, which most reputable sites don't have. Also, the site seemed to have just popped up out of nowhere. Finally, the domain name was a collection of random characters instead of a descriptive term that explains the purpose of the product or service like DigitalParenting.com.

This site existed purely to capture payment information from unsuspecting online shoppers. Unfortunately it likely obtained information from many victims before it was ultimately shut down. Remember the adage: *If it seems too good to be true, it probably is.*

USE MODERN PAYMENT METHODS
WHENEVER POSSIBLE.

The payment industry has changed significantly in the last decade. This is partly due to normal technological advancement, but it is also due to the nearly endless stream of data breaches that have exposed customers' credit card numbers. There was a time when I received a new credit or debit card almost monthly, due to the high number of data breaches at major retailers here in the United States.

Solutions like Apple Pay and Google Pay are more than just new ways to use your credit card on a mobile device: In many countries they shield your true account information by using virtual numbers. This means that they can either use a unique number for each transaction or they can just generate a new virtual card number if one of them is included in a breach. While this feature isn't equally supported in all countries, using these services is safer than pulling out your physical card.

While I realize that this note goes beyond the bounds of our digital world, I'd like to add that in-person payments are also safer when leveraging modern methods like tap to pay or chip cards instead of swipe-based payments, which are prone to physical hacking vulnerabilities.

ONLY TRANSACT ON SECURE SITES.

Those first few letters in the address bar of your browser are extremely important. Sites that are only using *http* have an unencrypted connection. This means that anyone can read the information passing from your device to the website. This doesn't really matter if you are checking the weather, but it is potentially problematic if you are making an online purchase.

The risk here is much lower than it has ever been. More and more sites are using the encrypted version, *https*. Even though this may be a rare risk today, both you and your child should be able to quickly determine whether you have an encrypted connection to any website you visit. Only transact on sites that have an encrypted, secure connection.

Defend Your Data

It doesn't take a lot of effort to get people to care about their money, but it can be a lot more challenging to get people to have an equal level of concern for their data. Leaked personal data can cause you problems. In addition, digital mementos that are lost may be impossible to recover. If you have a plan for defending your data, you can make sure the worst doesn't happen to you. The following steps will help you do just that.

BACK UP WHAT IS IMPORTANT TO YOU.

Backing up data used to be more complex than it is today. You may already have access to a service or platform that enables you to back up all your important data without having to pay any additional fees. While you shouldn't trust your data to just anyone, Apple, Google, Amazon, and Microsoft all have ways to back up your data into the cloud. The advantage of using these services is that even if your home and all your devices were destroyed, your data would live on in the cloud.

BE CAREFUL WHO YOU GIVE YOUR INFORMATION TO.

Earlier in Facebook's life, it was common for apps built on the Facebook platform to request information from your personal account. It may have been a simple quiz to predict the type of person you would marry or an entertaining game you could play in your browser. Each of these experiences requested a good deal of information about you, including most of your profile information as well as your list of friends.

While Facebook no longer enables experiences built on its platform to access information in this way, scam impersonation profiles continue to be an issue on the platform . . . and many of them can trace the data back to what was received through those apps.

DON'T USE PUBLIC DEVICES OR NETWORKS WITHOUT PROTECTION.

Before mobile boarding passes became commonplace, travelers used hotel computers to print out their boarding passes for the trip home. Think about this for a minute: If they logged into their personal account with the airline they were flying on a public computer, what was the computer doing with that information? Was this login made available to the next user who sat down at that computer? How would you know for sure? Public devices can be a risk.

Imagine you've hit the data limit on your phone while traveling to a new city. You see a boutique coffee shop and decide to stop in, since they offer free Wi-Fi. You open your Wi-Fi settings, select a network, and then check your bank account balance. While this may seem harmless, it is dangerous. How dangerous? It can enable someone to send you malware, snoop on your online activities, and even impersonate reputable sites or platforms. When you don't know who is controlling the network, there is a risk to your personal information.

I'm not telling you to never use a hotel computer or public Wi-Fi. I've used both in the last year. But you will need to take additional steps to ensure you remain safe. One such tool is a virtual private network or VPN. While this tool can be used for nefarious purposes as well, it is a valuable tool to leverage if you know you will need to use public networks.

Verify Everything
Today's scam attempts continue to increase in both frequency and sophistication. I've personally known people who have lost money or even significant personal data by falling for these tricks. The best advice I can give anyone is to always be skeptical and to verify everything. If something seems important, take the extra step to verify its validity.

CHECK THE SOURCE.

One of the most common types of scams involves someone posing as a popular company. This could be your bank or an online service like Netflix, as in my example at the beginning of this chapter. You may get a message stating that your account has been put on hold or that a fraudulent charge has been made against your account. The scammers will usually want you to click on a link or call a specific phone number to get the issue resolved.

If you've received an email or text message that you are not sure is real, you need to go to the source. If your bank sends you an email about a potential fraudulent charge, ignore all of the contact information in the message: Go to your bank's website, then call the number listed on the official website. Let them know what happened and let them guide you to the appropriate department.

If you receive a message from an online service stating that your account has been put on hold, you can log into that service to see if that is indeed true. In every case, ignore the contact information and links in the suspicious message and go straight to the source.

ALWAYS CHECK THE DOMAIN.

If you get an email or a text message which includes a link, you can learn a lot about the validity of the request by looking at the domain name. While this shouldn't be your only tool, it can be a powerful one.

For the purposes of this example, let's say that you bank at Bank of America. One morning you receive a notification message claiming to be from your bank. You can immediately scan the email for a few things. First, did the email come from someone at bankofamerica.com? Next, if you hit the *reply* button, does it go to someone at bankofamerica.com, or does it go to a different domain? While there are ways for scammers to pretend to be sending you a message from another domain, they cannot hack the email address you will be replying to.

When checking the domain name, be sure to check that it isn't a misspelling of the real domain name, such as bankoamerica.com. Hackers have been known to use this trick too.

ACTION PLAN
Online Resources: https://dp.run/step6

This chapter has offered practices that you can follow to minimize the impact of online dangers to your family. Before we get to the Action Plan, I want to define the goal that we are working toward in this chapter:

Goal: To enable each member of your family to protect their privacy, data, and personal resources while online.

To achieve this goal, you will focus on two areas: implementing these practices in your own life and then teaching them to your child. The online resources for this chapter will walk you through implementing these practices. Because they change so frequently, we will be continually updating those resources to deal with emerging dangers.

One difference between this step and the previous steps in this book is that you won't be able to complete this Action Plan within a week or even a month. Your goal should be to improve your online safety bit by bit over a handful of months. Incremental improvements with these practices can greatly reduce the risk you and your family face online.

Don't forget to update your Action Plan Tracker as you go.

1. IMPLEMENT SECURITY AND PRIVACY PRACTICES
FOR ALL FAMILIES

Unless you work in a technology-related field, there were likely some concepts in this chapter that made you realize the need to improve how you maintain your own online privacy and security. Take the time to identify a handful of critical areas where you need to implement these practices. If you have questions on how to implement one of the practices, please post it to the *Digital Parenting Community* and we will be sure to respond.

Additional information on how to adopt these practices in your own life can be found in the online resources for this chapter.

2. EDUCATE YOUR CHILD ON THE SECURITY AND PRIVACY PRACTICES
FOR FAMILIES WITH CHILDREN CURRENTLY USING DEVICES

As your child engages in the digital world, you will have a chance to teach them these concepts as they need them. Unlike some of the other steps, you won't be able to sit down and cover every single principle in one sitting. Instead, plan to teach these practices incrementally. In the online resources for this chapter we recommend specific ages for each principle, but you will need to use your own best judgment for your child.

A tracking worksheet is provided in the online resources for this chapter. You can use it to note which practices you've already covered with your child.

11

STEP 7

Consuming Critically

And it is my prayer that your love may abound more and more, with knowledge and all discernment, so that you may approve what is excellent, and so be pure and blameless for the day of Christ. (PHILIPPIANS 1:9-10)

ON FEBRUARY 12, 2023, a group of students from George Fisher Middle School in Putnam County, New York, opened TikTok to find something completely unexpected. It was a video of their principal engaging in a racist tirade. The video ended with him saying he would bring his machine gun to school, and he insinuated that he planned to use it on the school's Black students. On the same day another video appeared on the platform, showing a member of local law enforcement continuing the racist tirade with his own threats.

You would have been outraged at the comments and threats made through these videos, but there is something else you need to know: *These videos weren't real.* They were created by students at a nearby high school, using new AI-based technologies. These technologies enable creators to take an existing video and modify it, so it appears as if it were someone else.[1] These videos, commonly called *deepfakes*, have become increasingly lifelike.

Today's media presents additional risks beyond fake videos. On the one hand, all of us are continual marketing targets. Everywhere we go online, we are presented with products, services, and solutions that claim to make our lives better, easier, and more luxurious. When it comes to the news, there is a steady stream of information, but the days of unbiased journalism are mostly over. As an adult, you may have built mental protections to identify these ulterior motives, but what about your child?

In today's digital world, your child will have to analyze the validity of more media than any prior generation ever has. Each media message has its own agenda. Anyone operating in this digital world needs to have the ability to clearly distinguish between what is real and fake as well as between what is right and wrong. Before diving into the existing dangers and corresponding Action Plan, let's revisit the biblical concept that describes this ability: *discernment.*

DISCERNMENT

When Paul was writing his letter to the church at Philippi, he included his prayer for them. He prayed that their love would abound more and more, and then he said something interesting. He prayed that

---

1   David Gilbert, "High Schoolers Made a Racist Deepfake of a Principal Threatening Black Students," *Vice*, March 8, 2023. http://www.vice.com/en/article/7kxzk9/school-principal-deepfake-racist-video.

they would have this love with "knowledge and all discernment." Paul doesn't wait long to explain why he added this. He says that they need knowledge and discernment to "approve what is excellent" and to "be pure and blameless."[2]

Discernment is knowing the difference between what is excellent and what is not. The things that are excellent should be approved, and the things that are not should never be approved. Without discernment, we are stuck without the ability to determine which is which. In a world that changes as rapidly as ours, this can be a very dangerous thing.

In some ways we have been talking about discernment throughout this entire book, but I want to focus on it explicitly here. It has never been easier to connect with people with different worldviews. It has never been easier to publish or consume new ideas. It has never been easier to come across ideas that run contrary to the Bible and God's will for us as Christians.

If I were to paraphrase Paul's words here, I would say that he wanted to be sure the Philippian Christians were not easily fooled or unknowingly influenced by false ideas and doctrine. He wanted their love to be anchored in an understanding of the truth. When it comes to the modern barrage of messages sent to today's youth through Netflix series, YouTube ads, movies, and TikTok influencers, it is just as critical for them to be able to use discernment in evaluating these messages. It is part of your parenting mandate to anchor your child in the truth, so that they aren't constantly bouncing from one new idea to the next, with no anchor to secure them.[3]

DANGERS

The dangers of media consumption may not even register on your radar when it comes to technology risks. But I want to remind you that few

---

2   See Phil 1:9–10.

3   See Eph 4:14.

things have the power to shift your child's worldview more than this. If you want to raise your child to be able to stand firm in God in this current culture, you have to take an active role in shaping how they consume and process the information that is presented to them.

Take a moment to remember those *wants* you identified in your parenting blueprint and consider how they could be affected by the media your child consumes.

Dissatisfaction

In 2021 companies around the globe spent more than half a trillion dollars on digital advertising.[4] To put that into context, that is more money than the size of the entire economy for countries like Ireland, New Zealand, or Norway.[5] While a majority of this money targets adults, an ever-increasing percentage of it is targeted at today's youth.

When I was a teen, it was relatively easy to discern what was and what was not advertising. Thirty-second commercials during my favorite shows, full-page ads in the daily newspaper, and that quick reminder in the movie theater to buy popcorn before the show were all obviously advertisements. There was a clear distinction between entertainment and the sales pitch. In our digital world, however, these lines have been blurred.

Much of the content on YouTube, TikTok, and Instagram contains paid product placement, even if the creator does not disclose it. Even overt paid ads on platforms like Facebook, X (formerly known as Twitter), and Google are made to blend in with other content. While there is usually a small indicator that the result or post is sponsored, it looks very similar to any other post.

---

4   Sara Lebow, "Worldwide Digital Ad Spend Will Top $600 Billion This Year," *Insider Intelligence*, January 31, 2023. http://www.insiderintelligence.com/content/worldwide-digital-ad-spend-will-top-600-billion-this-year.

5   "World Economic Outlook Database," International Monetary Fund, October 2021, https://www.imf.org/en/Publications/WEO/weo-database/2021/October/weo-report.

When you pair this ever-increasing budget for online advertising with how well camouflaged it is in the content your child is consuming, it becomes challenging for them to see it for what it is. Most adults have developed some mental protections against advertising, but in young people these skills are still developing. When we realize someone is trying to sell us something, we listen more critically. However, when a friend simply tells us about a new product they enjoy, we let down our guard. This scenario is exactly what advertisers actively seek to exploit in many of our online interactions.

So, what's the danger in rampant hidden advertising bombarding your child at every point? Let me ask you this: If they didn't know about the latest clothing trend, gadget, or accessory, would they obsess over it? Probably not. Advertising, by its very nature, gives birth to materialism, especially when we don't see it for what it is. Materialism, if left unchecked, wages war on our spiritual health. A study from 2012 showed a connection between exposure to television advertising and lower life satisfaction:

> It is plausible that the material values portrayed in advertising teach children that material possessions are a way to cope with decreased life satisfaction . . . findings among adults suggest that materialistic children may become less happy later in life.[6]

I'll venture to suggest that things on the materialism front haven't improved by the shift from the living room television set to our personal smartphones. Today's youth are encountering more ads in more places more often, and the result is increased levels of materialism for the masses. While you can't eliminate this danger, you can lessen its effects on your child by equipping them to identify every time they are being targeted by ads.

---

6   Suzanna J. Opree et al., "Lower Life Satisfaction Related to Materialism in Children Frequently Exposed to Advertising," *Pediatrics* 130, no. 3 (2012): e486–e491. doi:10.1542/peds.2011-3148.

The Wrong Discipleship

The concept of celebrity has changed greatly over my lifetime. When I was a teen, the most famous actors and musicians seemed to live in another galaxy. Except for the occasional television or magazine interview, you really knew very little about them.

Our digital world has birthed something completely new: *the influencer*. Instead of being shut off from the world, these influencers open nearly every aspect of their lives through vlogging, podcasts, Pinterest boards, video shorts, tweets, and photos. With this all-access pass to their lives, something else is created: *trust*. 70% of teens say that they trust influencers over traditional celebrities.[7]

Influencers aren't all bad. There is a collection of people I follow in the tech, entrepreneurship, and ministry spaces that are considered influencers. The problem comes when these relationships supersede our actual in-person relationships. One study found that four in ten millennials say their favorite creator understands them better than their friends do.[8] In many cases this is because the influencer is having an ongoing one-way conversation with the viewer that is shaping the way the viewer sees the world.

Passionately following an influencer is a type of digital discipleship. In March of 2022, *The Babylon Bee*, a Christian satirical news site, posted an article titled, *Parents Baffled That 1 Hour of Youth Group A Week Not Effectively Combating Teen's 30 Hours On TikTok*.[9] If you

7   "20 Surprising Influencer Marketing Statistics," *Digital Marketing Institute* (blog), October 19, 2021, http://www.digitalmarketinginstitute.com/blog/20-influencer-marketing-statistics-that-will-surprise-you.

8   "Why YouTube Stars Are More Influential Than Traditional Celebrities," Think with Google, Accessed April 23, 2023, https://www.thinkwithgoogle.com/_qs/documents/604/youtube-stars-influence-b.pdf.

9   "Parents Baffled That 1 Hour of Youth Group A Week Not Effectively Combating Teen's 30 Hours On TikTok," Babylon Bee, March 17, 2022, https://babylonbee.com/news/parents-baffled-that-1-hour-of-youth-group-a-week-not-effectively-combating-teens-30-hours-on-tiktok.

work in youth ministry, you likely feel the pain as you read this headline. Many teens know more about Charli D'Amelio than they do about Jesus. While screen time limits greatly minimize the effects of these outside influences, we still need to teach that our primary calling is to be a disciple of Jesus and not a disciple of this world.

As parents, we must take time to discuss current events and the important topics of the day with our kids. This will be a part of the Action Plan in this chapter. Part of the reason that this is essential is because of the power that influencers wield when it comes to worldview. While you may feel that your child is insulated from a specific event or topic, it is likely that many influencers are evangelizing their own worldview regarding that specific issue. I recommend that you strive to be the first and not the second, third, or fourth place your child hears about a contentious idea or topic.

Echo Chambers

Our current social media landscape tends to create pockets of people with similar interests and worldviews. A quick scroll through available Facebook Groups will highlight fans of niche sports, owners of specific goat breeds, and fans of specific sci-fi series. Concurrently, something else is happening at a deeper level. Due to a combination of our preferences and the algorithms used by social media platforms, we can find ourselves surrounded by people who think a lot like us. This might not seem like a problem, but this results in *echo chambers*:

> In news media and social media, an echo chamber is an environment or ecosystem in which participants encounter beliefs that amplify or reinforce their preexisting beliefs by communication and repetition inside a closed system and insulated from rebuttal.[10]

---

10 Wikipedia. "Echo chamber (media)." Accessed April 20, 2023. https://en.wikipedia.org/wiki/Echo_chamber_(media).

In some ways, this sounds ideal. You don't have to put up with people who view the world differently! While you may want to keep your younger child in a bit of an ideological bubble, God doesn't call them to stay there forever. If they stay there too long, they may be less capable of dealing with the worldviews they will encounter in the real world. We are called to engage with those who view the world differently, just as Paul engaged the Greek philosophers of the day at the Areopagus.[11]

In the first season of *The Rabbit Hole*, a documentary podcast from The New York Times, the host follows Caleb Caine, a twenty-six-year-old college dropout from West Virginia.[12] There was a period in Caleb's life when he was voraciously consuming content on YouTube. After he finished watching one video, he was immediately pulled into the other videos YouTube was recommending for him. Initially the algorithm led him down the path of the far-right political viewpoint. As he continued to watch, it seemed that the material he was viewing got more and more extreme without offering any differing or contrasting viewpoints.

Eventually, Caleb came across some differing viewpoints on another platform. When he searched for more of this content on YouTube, he ended up going down another algorithm-driven path that led him to even more extreme far-left viewpoints. In a relatively short period of time, the algorithm that powers YouTube had played a part in leading him to radical views on opposing ends of the political spectrum. As he pushed more into YouTube, he also pulled away from real-life relationships and interactions that could have helped him interpret and balance the content he was consuming online.

Unless we have a firm foundation in Christ, the algorithms that control the content we see will have great power in shaping our ideas.

---

11 See Acts 17:16–34.

12 Kevin Roose, host, "Three: Mirror Image," Rabbit Hole, episode 3, *The New York Times*, April 30, 2020, http://www.nytimes.com/2020/04/30/podcasts/rabbit-hole-internet-youtube-virus.html.

While Caleb's case deals mainly with his perception and worldview, many others have gone down these paths with much more dangerous results. This brings us to one of the dangerous outcomes of echo chambers: *radicalization*.

Radicalization

A 2022 study in the United Kingdom found that most people currently jailed for terrorism in England and Wales were "radicalised at least in part online.[13]" In previous generations, it was virtually impossible for young people to have a conversation with a terrorist network, but in our digital world, this is within the realm of possibility. Groups such as the Islamic State use online interactions as a key element of their overall recruitment strategy.

While the Internet is not the primary cause of radicalization, it has made it possible for a larger group of people to be influenced. The use of online platforms, paired with echo chambers, can create environments that are ripe for radicalization. Thankfully, if you have completed your Action Plan for Step 4, you have already limited the ability for some of these forces to contact your child directly.

SMART MEDIA PRINCIPLES

Most highways in the United States have guardrails that protect us from careening off a cliff or driving into a lake. When it comes to media, we also need guardrails. We need these barriers to ensure that we know the difference between reality and fiction. We also need to navigate the constant minefield of marketing tactics. The following Smart Media Principles can help your child, but they are also designed to help humans of any age navigate the constant barrage of media influence in our digital world.

---

13 Vikram Dodd, "Most Convicted Terrorists Radicalised Online, Finds MoJ-Backed Study," *The Guardian*, December 8, 2022, https://www.theguardian.com/uk-news/2022/dec/08/most-convicted-terrorists-radicalised-online-finds-study.

The information in the first principle, *Understand*, is the foundation your child needs to know. In the next two principles, *Assess* and *Verify*, your child will gain techniques they can leverage to determine the value of any content they encounter.

Understand

The first step toward empowering your child to critically examine the information they will encounter is to teach them some core truths about our digital world. These can be used to help them analyze any media they evaluate.

UNDERSTAND THAT INFORMATION ONLINE CAN OFTEN BE MISLEADING OR FAKE.

When I was in elementary school, I remember looking at some of the outlandish tabloids while waiting with my mom in the check-out line at the supermarket. The tabloids were pretty easy to spot, and the ridiculous headlines made it fairly clear which periodicals were legitimate and which were mostly fake. The Internet makes it more challenging to tell the difference between real information and misleading content.

The advances in AI and machine learning compound this problem. As discussed earlier in this chapter, we can no longer assume that a video is clear proof of truth. With continual improvements to tools which can modify images, audio, and video content, we must all become more discerning when it comes to determining whether specific media can be trusted or not.

UNDERSTAND THAT COMPANIES AND CREATORS ARE ALWAYS MARKETING TO YOU.

Most young people I've spoken with don't understand the efforts that are being made to continually sell products, ideas, and services to them. They are not yet perceptive enough to spot every paid product placement on TikTok and YouTube. They don't yet understand that their desire for a product is the result of an expertly crafted marketing campaign. To survive and be content in this digital world, your child will need to know that they are being targeted by advertising almost every minute they are online.

While steps have been taken through various laws in multiple countries to force online creators to state when they are being paid to market a specific product, these steps are not always followed. Additionally, it might not be obvious to your child unless they read through the complete description for each video they watch or every podcast they listen to. It is important for your child to understand that advertising still pays for most of the content they watch online, whether they realize it or not.

UNDERSTAND THAT COMPANIES DECIDE WHAT YOU SEE ON SOCIAL MEDIA AND WHICH RESULTS COME UP IN SEARCH ENGINES.

Whether we are on YouTube, TikTok, Facebook, or even Instagram, our experiences are manipulated. These online platforms as well as many others use algorithms to determine what content you see and what content you don't. They do this because the more content you like and enjoy, the longer you will engage with the platform. The longer you engage with the platform, the more ads you'll see. The more ads you see, the more money the platforms make.

This engineered environment has several negative side effects. As discussed earlier, it can lead to echo chambers; in some cases it can even push someone to radically change their perspective on the world. To effectively see the whole picture, it may require breaking free from what the algorithm wants you to see by frequently disengaging from the platform altogether.

UNDERSTAND HOW SOCIAL NETWORKS AND SEARCH ENGINES MAKE MONEY WITH YOUR DATA.

One of the ways to help your child understand their digital world is to help them see how these *free* platforms actually make their money. Most popular online platforms make money through advertisements. For example, if you were launching a new fitness studio with childcare in Atlanta, you may want to target a specific demographic with advertising. On some platforms you can be as specific as saying you want to send your ads to moms between the ages of twenty-six and thirty-five in the greater Atlanta area who are into fitness. This level of sophistication can demand a premium from advertisers; the more the platforms know about their users, the more money they make.

When your child understands how these platforms monetize their experience, they will have more context, understand why they are seeing the ads they are seeing, and be better equipped to deal with the information they are presented on these platforms. They will also understand that these platforms aren't truly *free*, as we are *paying* for them with our personal data for the purposes of targeted advertising.

Verify

In Step 6 we focused on practices that enable us to operate online safely. Part of that was knowing how to validate and verify the messages and emails we receive. The following group of concepts extends that idea by applying it to how we verify all of the media we consume. Whether it is a social media post, a news story, or even a shared photo, we need tools to help us to distinguish what is real from what is not.

VERIFY THAT THE INFORMATION IS FROM A REPUTABLE SOURCE.

I don't want to be in the business of rating media outlets for reliability, but not all sources should be trusted. A large, established news company has more at stake than some random blog that launched two days ago. As your child gets into their mid- and late-teen years, I recommend giving your child some news sources that you think are best for them to use.

Part of this analysis of articles and videos they discover online is to analyze the URL. This is a similar concept to what was covered in Step 6 when we were analyzing steps to prevent scams. A hacker could copy the websites for the BBC, CNN, and The New York Times, but cannot clone their URLs.[14] If we see a domain or subdomain with a bunch of random characters instead of a descriptive domain name, we can be fairly certain that it isn't a reliable source.

CHECK MULTIPLE SOURCES.

Few celebrities have been killed off in social media as many times as Morgan Freeman has. After one incident he famously stated, "Like Mark Twain, I keep reading that I have died. I hope those stories are not true…"[15] Because of the speed of social media, many of us desire to share information as quickly as possible. This has often led to untrue reports going viral.

To help combat the spread of false information, I recommend you teach your child to verify information with multiple sources, especially before they share the story with anyone else. While this may mean that they aren't the first to post about an event, it will help them to fulfill their calling to speak truth and wisdom instead of folly. It will also give their posts more weight, allowing their contacts to see them as a trusted source.

---

14 While there are technically ways to do this if you fully control a network, this is beyond what your children need to consider.

15 Morgan Freeman, "Responding to Online Reports of His Death," *Facebook*, October 23, 2012, http://www.facebook.com/MorganFreeman/posts/like-mark-twain-i-keep-reading-that-i-have-died-i-hope-those-stories-are-not-tru/373897579359566/.

Assess

After your child understands the realities of the media-driven world and has verified the source of the information, the next step is to assess the quality of the content itself.

ASSESS THE COMPLETE INFORMATION.

In our digital world significant efforts are made to get viewers to click on a headline, thumbnail image, or social media post. These are often exaggerated, and they may not be true to the actual content. In many cases, the article's author has little or no input on these "hooks." I recommend you teach your child to look deeper than these deceptive headlines if they truly want to understand what the information is about.

It is commonplace for people to share something online before they have analyzed its entire content. If we don't have the time or desire to use our critical thinking skills to analyze a piece of media, this should be a sign to us that it isn't worth sharing. Since we have a biblical calling to present those around us with wisdom, this analysis becomes an essential step before we click that *share* button.

ASSESS THE PURPOSE OF THE INFORMATION.

One superpower you can give your child is the ability to understand the *why* of the information they consume. Some media exists to simply entertain, but that is rarer than many of us realize. Most media exists to persuade people to purchase a product, adopt a viewpoint, or take action in some way. If you can teach your child to discern the purpose of each message for themselves, they can avoid the traps many others fall into.

ASSESS WHETHER THE INFORMATION ALIGNS WITH GOD'S WORD.

As a part of discipleship, I recommend you teach your child to spot what does and does not align with God's word. Unlike previous generations, we cannot simply isolate our kids from information that goes against a Christian worldview. Instead, we must teach them to identify it. We need to give them resources for analyzing any media they encounter in light of the Bible.

ACTION PLAN
Online Resources: https://dp.run/step7

While the dangers are real, there *is* a way to provide your child with a foundation that will give them tools to deal with what they will encounter. First, I want to provide a goal that will serve as a guide as we walk through this Action Plan:

GOAL: To enable your child to critically analyze the media they consume by thoughtfully evaluating their source, meaning, and purpose.

By equipping your child with a firm foundation, teaching them to leverage the Smart Media Principles, and maintaining the other guidelines in this book, you can provide them with the best defense against the ever-present challenges posed by our modern media.

At DigitalParenting.com we are continually providing new tools and resources to help you educate your child on our Smart Media Principles. Be sure to thoroughly review the online resources for this chapter before diving in to complete the Action Plan.

While teaching these principles initially may take a few weeks, learning to use them effectively will require some follow-up with your child.

Because of this, we provide recommendations for how often we think you should revisit these concepts in your home. Don't forget to mark off your completed tasks on your Action Plan Tracker as you go along.

1. COMPLETE THE BIBLE STUDY ON DISCERNMENT WITH YOUR CHILD
FOR FAMILIES WITH CHILDREN AGES 7+

As part of your ongoing discipleship effort, you will need to teach your child about the biblical concept of discernment. This study will enable you to define it, describe where it comes from, and explain how it should be used as they navigate online content. It is my hope that this study will help them understand the power and ability given to them by the Holy Spirit to tell the difference between wisdom and folly; right and wrong.

The Bible study guide on discernment is available in the online resources for this chapter.

2. TALK THROUGH THE SCENARIOS IN THE DISCUSSION GUIDE USING THE SMART MEDIA PRINCIPLES
FOR FAMILIES WITH CHILDREN AGES 9+

The discussion guide, which is included in the online resources for this chapter, provides scenarios that you can use to discuss these media principles with your child. You can define the overall principles, then encourage your child to apply this knowledge to scenarios that are based on real-life situations. By asking them what they would do in a specific scenario, they are given the opportunity to carefully think through how they will respond before they have to make that decision in real life.

Just as was the case in the previous step, the goal of these scenarios is to allow your child to practice these concepts and have some tools in hand before they encounter them in the real world.

This discussion guide is available in the online resources for this chapter.

3. PROVIDE A CHRISTIAN WORLDVIEW FOUNDATION FOR YOUR CHILD
FOR FAMILIES WITH CHILDREN AGES 7+

There are multiple experts that have written books, created courses, and even hosted conferences on helping children adopt a Christian worldview. The exact approach for how to teach and train your child on this worldview is beyond the scope of this book. That being said, I highly encourage you to put this on your radar for your child.

To help you in this area, we have provided a list of recommended resources that can help you teach a Christian worldview in your own home. Many of these resources are the ones we use in the Tucker household with our own children. It is a worthwhile and essential task, and that is the reason why it is included here. Even with the best tools and techniques, our judgment can falter without a strong foundation.

Recommended resources for teaching a Christian worldview can be found in the online resources for this chapter.

PART III

Getting Answers

12

Should I Get Professional Help?

Online Resources: https://dp.run/ch12

I HOPE THE INFORMATION contained in *The 7 Essential Steps of Digital Parenting* has been helpful for you. I have seen it be life-changing for families. I get excited every day when I think of families that will grow closer, teens that will have a deeper relationship with God, and future marriages that will become stronger because of the steps taken upon reading this book. These reasons encourage me daily as I work on DigitalParenting.com.

However, some of you may have had a different experience. You may have met with significant resistance from your child while trying to implement your Action Plan. The longer your child has been using devices, the higher the likelihood you will encounter opposition from them throughout the application of the principles in this book.

There are many side effects of device usage that are true clinical conditions. Issues like addiction, depression, anxiety, and trauma are real and may require the help of a mental health professional or physician.

How do you know when to consult a professional? Unfortunately, there is no universal answer to that question. As a parent, you must use your best judgment. If you feel that your child's use of technology is negatively affecting their life and interfering with their ability to function, you should consider seeing a professional. If you have observed erratic behavior, violent opposition to the monitoring of their devices, or abrupt social aversion, you should seek professional intervention.

Even though I will give you a tool that will provide you with a list of behavioral areas to analyze in your child, this tool should not take the place of your parental instinct. If you feel that your child has a legitimate need in this area, I recommend seeking out the help of a professional. In this chapter I want to walk you through some areas to consider as well as some steps to follow to find a mental health professional for your child if you decide to do so.

ASSESSING THEIR SCREEN USE

The Problematic Media Use Measure is a tool that was created by a group of academics from the University of Michigan, Central Michigan University, and Iowa State University.[1] The authors span multiple disciplines including medicine, psychology, and communications. This tool has been designed to provide insight into screen addiction for children from ages four to eleven, but the tool can also be helpful when analyzing your child's screen time, even if they are older than the target age.

While I won't be walking you through a formal use of the tool, I believe the questions it asks will help inform your judgment. Parents too often assume that their child's struggles with screen time are normal, when in some cases specific behaviors indicate that a serious problem has developed.

Problematic Media Use Measure

The Problematic Media Use Measure consists of twenty-seven

---

1   Sarah E. Domoff et al., "Development and Validation of the Problematic Media Use Measure: A Parent Report Measure of Screen Media 'Addiction' in Children," *Psychology of Popular Media Culture* 8, no. 1 (2019): 2–11. doi:10.1037/ppm0000163.

questions covering specific behavioral concerns related to screen time addiction. I would recommend finding some uninterrupted time when you can thoughtfully analyze your child's behavior in relation to the statements below. As you ponder each statement, score your child's behavior on a scale of 1 (Never) to 5 (Always).

A score sheet for the Problematic Media Use Measure is included in the online resources for this chapter.

1. It is hard for my child to stop using screen media.

2. It is increasingly difficult to pull my child away from screen media.

3. It is really difficult to get my child to stop using screen media.

4. Screen media is the only thing that seems to motivate my child.

5. My child is always thinking about using screen media.

6. Screen media is all that my child seems to think about.

7. My child becomes frustrated when he/she cannot use screen media.

8. My child's screen media use interferes with family activities.

9. My child gets upset when he/she cannot use screen media.

10. There is nothing my child enjoys as much as screen media.

11. My child becomes angry when he/she cannot use screen media.

12. My child's screen media use causes problems for the family.

13. The amount of time my child wants to use screen media keeps increasing.

14. My child attempts to use screen media for increasing amounts of time.

15. Problems occur for our family when my child cannot use screen media.

16. My child would find life boring without screen media.

17. Life would be easier if my child was not so attached to screen media.

18. The first thing my child asks to do when he/she comes home from school is to use screen media.

19. My child's screen media use negatively affects his/her friendships.

20. My child uses screen media for increasing amounts of time.

21. My child loses sleep due to screen media use.

22. My child sneaks using screen media.

23. My child lies about doing chores or schoolwork in order to use screen media.

24. When my child has had a bad day, screen media seems to be the only thing that helps him/her feel better.

25. My child feels better when he/she uses screen media.

26. My child uses screen media to feel better.

27. My child lies in order to use screen media.

Your score on this exercise may rank anywhere from 27 to 135. The higher the score, the higher your level of concern should be for your child's screen use. That being said, not all of the items here are equal. If your child frequently lies in order to use screen media (question 27), you may want to see a professional, even if all of the other items have a low score. As I said earlier, this is where your parental judgment comes into play.

FINDING A PROFESSIONAL

At the time I am writing this chapter, there is a major shortage of mental health professionals in the United States. As depression, anxiety, and addiction have become more common, the number of professionals has not increased to meet the demand. This leaves many families wondering where to turn if they feel like their child has a legitimate need for support in this area. What should you do if you find yourself in this situation?

First, I would recommend bringing these concerns up with your child's physician. While we generally think that there is a clear separation between the issues physical and mental health providers address, physicians are starting to address some of the concerns that are caused by devices and screen time, too. In some situations, your physician might recommend treatment to address the issue. Even if your concern falls outside of their area of expertise, they can recommend a mental health professional. In many cases, you will be seen faster with a physician's referral than if you simply tried to schedule an appointment yourself.

Your church may have a list of mental health professionals they can recommend, so checking with your local church may be a good first step. This can be a quick way to find professionals who can provide Christian counseling.

If you still need assistance in finding a mental health professional, there are sites that provide directories you can use. One of the great benefits of technology is that virtual visits are now a reality. If there are no mental health providers available in your area, this may be a possible alternative to help your child recover from their addiction to screen time.

Please visit our online resources for this chapter for detailed information on how to find mental health professionals. These resources include information on directories and services we can recommend as well as a few warnings regarding some we cannot.

13

When Should I Get My Child a Phone?

Online Resources: https://dp.run/ch13

BY FAR THE MOST COMMON QUESTION I have received in my years of talking about Digital Parenting is, "When should I get my child a phone?" Answering this question has become a parental rite of passage in our digital world. I understand that there is immense pressure from your child, schools, and even other parents to put a smartphone in your child's hands. Rather than simply succumbing to their expectations, I want to help you make an informed and intentional decision for your family that lines up with the *wants* in your parenting blueprint.

WHAT NOT TO DO

Have you ever looked at how other parents handle a situation with their kids and thought, "Wow. They are going to regret that move." I've thought that many times as I've watched families at church, in the airport, or even at a local restaurant. While it's currently popular for parents to spend time and energy criticizing each other, as Christians we are called to encourage and support one another as we raise our children according to God's standards.

I've tried to present all the information in this book without judgment . . . and the same applies to this chapter. I don't want you to feel any judgment as I go through the common mistakes I've seen families make in this area. Even if you've already given your child a phone, it isn't too late to take it back. If you haven't yet given your child a phone, I hope these observations will guide you in the decision you need to make for them. Don't just give your child a phone because their friends or classmates have phones.

Phones seem to spread like a pandemic amongst youth groups, schools, and friend groups. Once one student gets a phone, those closest to them begin the campaign to convince their parents to get them one too. Before long the social setting for this group has completely changed, and the interactions now primarily happen online instead of in-person. I have seen even well-meaning parents cave when it comes to a relentless child begging for an iPhone.

I hope that I have given you enough information about the risks associated with devices that you already know that peer pressure and envy are not good enough reasons for your child to get a phone. As we have seen in many cases, their lives could be forever changed—or even lost—if they are simply given a phone without adequate guidance.

I am a firm believer that children should not have a smartphone before the age of fourteen unless there is a specific reason for them to have one. During my years of working on this topic, I haven't seen as many *valid* reasons as you might expect.

DON'T GIVE THEM A SMARTPHONE WITHOUT CONSIDERING OTHER OPTIONS FIRST.

I couldn't imagine giving any of my kids a Ferrari for their first car. Its capabilities, dangers, and cost make it an illogical place to start. Far too many parents immediately jump to a smartphone as their child's first phone. This could be an iPhone, Google Pixel, or Samsung Galaxy. While there aren't as many beginner options for phones as there are for cars, there are viable alternatives that should be considered first. I often hear, "I need to be able to get in touch with my child." There are far safer ways to stay connected with your child than jumping immediately into a full-featured smartphone.

There are old-school phones (often called feature phones), smart watches, and even smartphones that have been modified to limit which actions your child can take. In each case, these are better options for *first* phones than a fully featured smartphone. Take time to ask yourself, "What specific features does my child actually need?" Chances are you can find something that is suited to your use case that isn't a smartphone.

Please visit the online resources for this chapter to see an up-to-date list of smartphone alternatives for your child.

DON'T GIVE THEM A PHONE WITHOUT ANY GUIDANCE, TRAINING, OR BOUNDARIES.

If you have already completed this book and its accompanying online resources, you already have what you need to establish the proper guidance, training, and boundaries for your child. You are already miles ahead of parents who haven't been through this material.

But before you hand your child that phone, you need to ask yourself: Do you currently have the time to invest in properly training and equipping your child? Do you know how you will set up screen time limits and content filtering for their device? Will you have the conversations outlined in the Action Plans for each step to ensure that they will be able to deal with what they may encounter online?

If the answer to any of these questions is *no*, you shouldn't give your child a phone yet. There are seasons of life when busyness takes over, and both you and your child would benefit from waiting until you have the proper amount of time to equip them with the tools they need.

DON'T GIVE THEM A PHONE IF THEY AREN'T MATURE ENOUGH TO UNDERSTAND THE ATTENDING DANGERS.

If you walked through the halls of any elementary school in the United States today, you would likely be amazed at the number of kids carrying phones. By the age of ten, 42% of children already have a smartphone.[1] If you feel that you cannot trust your child to care for a device worth hundreds of dollars, or if you don't think they are mature enough to deal with the challenges they could face online, they shouldn't have a phone. I have yet to meet a ten-year-old who fully meets these criteria.

OUR PLANS

While your decision on when to get your child a phone is yours, I did want to share what we are currently doing and what we plan to do in the Tucker home. As I'm writing this chapter, I have three young teenagers at home. While they are each responsible for an iPad they use for their schooling, they do not have their own phones. This is by design.

My children are getting closer to the age when we will begin to teach them how to drive. Our plan is that they will have a phone when they turn sixteen, which is when they are allowed to get a driver's license in our state. When my wife and I examined the dangers of devices alongside our desire to train our children to be self-sufficient adults, this seemed like the right age to begin training them on how to responsibly own and use a phone.

My kids have plenty of friends who have phones, but they also have friends who do not. We have explained to them that Jesus has called us to live countercultural lives, and that this is an area where they will be different, even from some of their friends at church. We have had regular discussions with them on this over the past five years, so there

---

1   Rideout et al., *Common Sense Census.*

was no expectation that they would have a phone the moment their friends got one. Because we set the expectation early, this hasn't been a recurring argument in our home.

YOUR PLAN

I don't expect you to simply adopt our approach. I have spoken with a lot of families over the past five years, and their circumstances have warranted different plans and approaches. I've spoken with families who are co-parenting, sending their child to boarding school, and foster parenting. Each of these situations presents a unique set of challenges that needs to be addressed in its own way.

While there have been justified reasons for giving a child a phone earlier than I recommend, I am still adamant about one thing: If you don't have the time to properly train, protect, and equip your child to use a phone wisely, you should not get them a phone.

14

What Comes Next?

Before you set this book down, I must remind you that technology will continue to evolve, new dangers will continue to present themselves, and your child will still need your guidance. How can you continue to build on *The 7 Essential Steps of Digital Parenting*? That's what I'll address in this chapter.

TYING UP LOOSE ENDS

First, there are some of you who may have skipped specific steps in the Action Plan because your child was not yet of the age where it made sense to cover the topic completely. Others of you may have tackled these items for one child but held off for a younger sibling. Revisit your Action Plan Tracker and determine what still needs to be completed for each child and when you plan to do it. Finally, I want you to put these dates into some task or reminder app, so that you'll get a gentle nudge once that date approaches. This will help to prevent your child from missing any of this important instruction.

Second, some of the topics covered in this book need to be revisited with your family on a recurring basis. Just because you covered a topic once, doesn't mean that your child has fully integrated its concepts into their life. I recommend that you not treat this as a one-and-done effort.

Third, some of you have big questions that have not been addressed in this book. This was partly by design. It is not possible to cover every digital parenting topic within these pages. This is why I created the *Digital Parenting Community*. If you want an answer on something like how to implement screen time settings on a Samsung Galaxy phone or how to best talk to your child about pornography, jump onto the community site. You can even ask for feedback from other parents on how to best tell your child that their digital life will look different from the digital lives of their friends. If you have any questions at all on digital parenting, drop them into our online community, and we will be sure to respond.

THE PATH TO MATURITY

As I walked through each of *The 7 Essential Steps of Digital Parenting*, I shared goals. My hope was that these goals would help you to focus on why that specific step was important in your life and the life of your child. Before we talk about a path to maturity for your child, I want to present a goal that I hope will guide your efforts as your child approaches adulthood.

To raise children into adults that can honor God with their digital lives.

When my children are in their twenties, we don't plan on setting their screen time limits, monitoring their digital activity, or limiting what apps can be installed on their phones. We want them to become adults who wisely manage their own digital lives. For that to happen, we will need to create a plan for how we will begin to transition areas of responsibility from us to them. This is their path to maturity. This is where we as parents will shift from rule makers to coaches.

We plan to begin this transition when our children are seventeen.

This will give us time to walk alongside our children as they live out the concepts we have taught them. We would rather our children make small mistakes when they are at home than make huge ones when they are out on their own. Their digital lives will be just one of many areas where they will be gaining new responsibilities at this age.

The path to maturity for your child will need to be a plan of your own creation. It requires you to know your child—their strengths, and their struggles. Just as with everything else in this book, I believe this needs to be an intentional plan. You will need to clearly identify which responsibilities will be transitioned to your child, and you will need to remind them what is at stake in their own lives.

CLOSING THOUGHTS

I pray that God will bless the efforts you have put into this material and that your family will escape the dangers that so many families are facing in our digital world. I also pray that you can set an example of thoughtful, disciplined, and wise use of technology for those around you.

Finally, I hope that you will continue to spread the news about DigitalParenting.com and this book to other families who could benefit from its content. I honestly believe that it is possible to raise a generation of Christian youth who will be spared the negative effects that result from using technology without guidance, limits, boundaries, or biblical discipleship.

ACKNOWLEDGMENTS

NO HUMAN has played as big a part in making this book a reality as my wife Shannon. She always encouraged me to pursue this project. She remains the first editor to review all my work, and she has greatly shaped how the information is structured within this book. I am so grateful for her love and support.

I can't say enough about the influence of my entire family. My dad provided me with a priceless example of Christlike living and the encouragement to pursue what I felt called to do. I still miss him every day. My mom continues to support my work, and I'm thankful she is integrated into the day-to-day for our family. I also have been greatly encouraged in all my personal and professional endeavors by my older brothers, Brian and Kevin, who provided an example for me to follow. My kids—Kaden, Keegan, and Brenna—have also supported this project by serving as test subjects for some of the approaches covered in this book and by putting up with an inordinate number of dad jokes.

This book would not have been possible without my church family at ChristWay Church in Ooltewah, TN. I especially want to thank John

Waters, Josh Cross, and the elders. For the past year barely a week has gone by when someone wasn't cornering me at church, asking me how they could help with DigitalParenting.com. Special thanks goes to all the families who provided valuable input during our initial focus groups at ChristWay to test out the material.

Dr. Mitchell Waters has been an advocate for DigitalParenting.com from the early days. I am grateful for his input on this book, his participation in our early events, and his willingness to be a sounding board for the mental health topics covered in our resources.

Few people were as involved in the early stages of this book as Andy Hughes, along with his wife Lindsay. As my co-leader for the very first focus group, Andy's feedback was vital. It was great to have another Christian father and technologist to chat with as I pondered what needed to go into this book.

I want to thank Christina Pfister (from Well Versed, LLC) for her contributions as the editor of this book. This book has been greatly improved by her recommendations.

Thank you to both Christian Saylor (from Ekko Studio) and Greg Reese (from Reese Creative) for their impact on the brand and positioning of DigitalParenting.com. Their collective excitement about my goals encouraged me to push through many difficult aspects of getting the organization launched.

Early on in DigitalParenting.com, I benefitted from the knowledge of a group of advisors including Nolan Rumble, Eric Frazier, Robby Campano, Brad Ruiter, Dr. Mitchell Waters, and Jay Mays. I want to thank you for providing input early in the DigitalParenting.com journey.

Finally, I want to add an additional word of thanks to Jay Mays. Many years ago, during a work event, he asked me what I would do if I could do anything. Even then I knew that DigitalParenting.com was both a passion and a calling, but his question and the ensuing conversation sparked something in me that led to this book. Thank you for your encouragement.